Biblical
Greek
Exegesis

Biblical Greek Exegesis

A Graded Approach to Learning
Intermediate and Advanced Greek

George H. Guthrie &
J. Scott Duvall

ZondervanPublishingHouse
Grand Rapids, Michigan

A Division of HarperCollins*Publishers*

Biblical Greek Exegesis
Copyright © 1998 by George H. Guthrie and J. Scott Duvall

Requests for information should be addressed to:

Zondervan Publishing House
Grand Rapids, Michigan 49530

ISBN 0-310-21246-4

Printed in the United States of America

98 99 00 01 02 03 04 /❖ VG/ 10 9 8 7 6 5 4 3 2 1

Dedication
To Those Who Taught Us Greek
At a Variety of Levels

David Irby
Hyran Barefoot
Thomas Urrey
Lorin Cranford
Douglas Moo
D. A. Carson
Jack W. MacGorman

Table of Contents

Section Two: The Exegetical Method

Acknowledgments

The completion of a project such as *Biblical Greek Exegesis* requires a chorus of coworkers. Those who taught us Greek, to whom this volume is dedicated, each contributed to our development in their own way. Lorin Cranford played a special role in laying a foundation for our approach to Greek pedagogy. In his Ph.D. seminar "New Testament Critical Methodologies," Dr. Cranford pushed us hard toward learning the content of the area but also forced us to grapple with the theory and practice of exegesis. In that seminar we also learned basic grammatical diagramming (which we have adapted to our own method).

Our good friend Bill Mounce opened himself to discussion about how our methodology might be included in *A Graded Reader of Biblical Greek*. After talks with Zondervan editors, we all agreed that the methodology needed to be presented in a separate volume, but Bill was the one who introduced our approach to the publisher. He has been a remarkable colleague as we have bounced ideas off of him, and he has become a friend for life. Also, the enthusiasm of our editors, Verlyn Verbrugge and Ed van der Maas, has kept us going. Verlyn's sharp eye and knowledge of New Testament Greek have provided keen insight to specific adjustments needed in the book. Thanks also should go to Stan Gundry, who saw the potential in our work from the beginning and gave the nod to a radically different approach to Greek pedagogy.

Paul Jackson has served as a significant player in the development of the book, spending long hours reading and editing. He also has used the methodology on both the intermediate and advanced Greek levels, and his feedback and suggestions have made their mark on the final product. Other field testers, to whom we are grateful, have also used the book in a provisional form and provided helpful comments.

What can we say about our students at Ouachita Baptist University and Union University? They have served as engaging "guinea pigs" as our methodology developed over the past several years. They have been patient in working with us and have made valuable suggestions too numerous to recount. Their perseverance in frustration and joy in discovery of the Greek text of the New Testament have provided the fundamental motivation for publication of this volume. They have encouraged us all along the way that this approach really does make a difference in Greek pedagogy. Our words cannot express adequately our love and appreciation for our students.

Finally, we must, as always, express deep appreciation for our families. Pat Guthrie and Judy Duvall, our wives, have been our most faithful supporters and exhorters in the development of this book. The Duvall children, Ashley, Amy, and Meagan, and the Guthrie children, Joshua and Anna, have kept us focused on the importance of family as our most immediate part of the body of Christ to whom we are called to minister. For all these friends and family members we give thanks to God, to whom be the glory. May this book work in some way to advance his kingdom through a more responsible study of his Word.

Preface for Teachers

THE NEED FOR A NEW APPROACH

If you are looking for a tool to use in teaching upper-level Greek that combines the study of syntax and diagramming with a comprehensive exegetical method, we invite you to consider *Biblical Greek Exegesis*. Using traditional methodology, many teachers move chapter by chapter through an upper-level grammar and have students do the exercises at the end of each chapter. The exercises normally require students to identify the syntactical function of elements within single verses pulled from different parts of the New Testament. Some teachers go a step further and supplement the grammar lesson with translation and syntax assignments from a single book of the New Testament, such as 1 John or Philippians. We are deeply grateful for such traditional approaches, and they certainly have much to commend them, but we have encountered serious pedagogical problems that limit their effectiveness with today's students. Before introducing our approach, we want to clarify what we mean when we speak of the "pedagogical problems" associated with many traditional methods.

First, traditional approaches often fail to motivate students, who tend to be more interested in understanding and applying the New Testament than in memorizing syntax categories. It usually takes several months just to cover the descriptions of the syntax possibilities, and by the end of this process students are overwhelmed with endless lists and their motivation is waning. They are disillusioned that they have yet to engage meaningfully larger portions of the New Testament in Greek—the reason they had taken the course in the first place.

Second, most traditional approaches are not "real world" in the sense of how students will engage New Testament Greek once course work is finished. Very few people who use the Greek New Testament in Christian ministry move from lists of syntax categories to the text. Rather, they begin with the text and use grammars and other reference works as tools to elucidate the text.

Third, the traditional approach risks divorcing the study of syntax from the overall process of understanding and applying the message of the New Testament. Students who labor through first-year Greek are eager to see firsthand the relevance of Greek for teaching and preaching. When the study of syntax is, for all practical purposes, isolated from the larger process of exegesis, students find it difficult to make the connection, and their desire to continue the rigors of Greek language study diminishes drastically.

Finally, restricting students to a micro-level analysis—focusing on words, phrases, clauses, and even sentences to the neglect of paragraphs and entire discourses—is perhaps the greatest single linguistic weakness of most contemporary approaches to teaching intermediate and advanced Greek.

Even the few problems mentioned above are pedagogically paralyzing for many of today's students. Most students are willing to invest the time necessary to learn the language if (and usually only if) they can see how the study of biblical Greek connects to life and ministry. In the next section we will survey a way of teaching intermediate and advanced Greek that builds on the strengths of traditional approaches and has worked well with our students. They are learning to integrate the study of Greek syntax into the larger enterprise of New Testament exegesis and they love it! At this point you might enjoy taking a look at the Preface for Students (see pp. 14–19).

THE APPROACH USED IN *BIBLICAL GREEK EXEGESIS*

Our enthusiasm about teaching biblical Greek runs high because we have had success in the classroom.[1] We are quick to acknowledge, however, that our success is due largely to the strength of our teaching method. Our students are willing and eager to pay the price in hours of study since they are convinced that a knowledge of Greek will help them in real-world ministry. We believe it takes more than an occasional pep talk about the relevance of Greek to convince students. As helpful as these might be (and we deliver our share of them), students need more. They need to see how the parts (such as identifying a certain kind of genitive) integrate into the larger task of moving from the ancient text to the modern audience. Our approach is intended to integrate the study of Greek into an overall exegetical method right from the beginning of intermediate Greek. We see our approach challenging and energizing our students, and we believe it will be equally motivating to students at other schools.

The title, *Biblical Greek Exegesis: A Graded Approach to Learning Intermediate and Advanced Greek*, draws attention to the two main parts of the work:

Section One focuses primarily on learning intermediate (or second-year) Greek syntax along with grammatical and semantic diagramming.

Section Two takes the student to the level of advanced (or third-year) Greek, incorporating their knowledge of syntax and diagramming into a comprehensive method of exegesis and exposition.

Let's look first at how we approach intermediate Greek.

Intermediate Greek

You could label our approach a *graded, modified-inductive* approach. Here's how it works. In the first-year course we both use Bill Mounce's *Basics of Biblical Greek*.[2] At the beginning of the second-year course, following a few class periods of orientation, students begin working in Section One of *Biblical Greek Exegesis*. Here we provide syntax and diagramming exercises for the following New Testament texts: 1 John 1:1–2:2; 2:28–3:10; John 15:1–27; Mark 1:1–28; Mark 8:27–9:8; Colossians 1:1–23; Matthew 6:5–34; Romans 3:21–26; 5:1–11; 8:1–17; James 1:1–21; and Philippians 1:27–2:13. These are the first nine passages in another book by Bill Mounce, *A Graded Reader of Biblical Greek*.[3]

We have divided these larger blocks of text into smaller units that can be covered in a week's time (usually about four to seven verses). We give students the assignment of translating the text, identifying the syntax of key terms, and diagramming a portion of the text. (A typical syntax assignment will include a mix of noun and verb forms.) We tell the students, "In addition to translating the passage and diagramming a portion of it, you are responsible for identifying the syntax of these terms (usually about eight to ten). After parsing each term, go to the summary sheet of syntax categories, see the possibilities, then come back and tell the class how you think each term functions syntactically in its context."[4] The strategy here is to get students to work *inductively* from the New Testament back to a consideration of syntax categories, the way they will approach the text in the real world.

During the class period for which the assignment is performed, the students share their answers to the exercises. Our task as teachers is to clarify the syntax categories in question and guide the students through the interpretive process. Over the course of their second year of study, students also build their own summary of syntax categories, all the while focusing on the text of the New Testament.

---

1. George Guthrie is Chair of the Department of Christian Studies at Union University in Jackson, Tennessee, and Scott Duvall is Associate Professor of Religion at Ouachita Baptist University in Arkadelphia, Arkansas. Both Ouachita and Union are Christian liberal arts universities that offer a major in Biblical Studies/Languages. As an example of the effectiveness of this approach, the total number of Greek students at Union University has grown from about thirty to ninety students in the last five years. Ouachita has experienced similar success.

2. William D. Mounce, *Basics of Biblical Greek: Grammar* (Grand Rapids: Zondervan, 1993).

3. William D. Mounce, *A Graded Reader of Biblical Greek* (Grand Rapids: Zondervan, 1996).

4. Part of the orientation includes supplying the students with a summary sheet of the syntax categories that includes brief definitions and examples from the New Testament. We highly recommend the summary in Daniel B. Wallace's *Greek Grammar Beyond the Basics: An Exegetical Syntax of the New Testament* (Grand Rapids: Zondervan, 1996), 726–69. For a partial summary of Wallace's *Greek Grammar*, see pp. 141–82 in Mounce's *Graded Reader*.

Periodically we review the syntax categories learned thus far and fill in the gaps by introducing the few categories not covered in the assigned passages. For this reason we describe the approach as a *modified*-inductive method.

Throughout the year the assignments get progressively longer and more difficult. Thus the approach is *graded*. In addition to translation and syntax, weekly assignments include diagramming and vocabulary exercises. Initially the students only do grammatical diagramming, but as time goes by they are taught to do semantic diagramming. Together, grammatical and semantic diagramming offer students a valuable tool for understanding the structure and meaning of paragraphs and entire discourses. Do not be overwhelmed by our diagramming methods. They may look complex at first glance, but consider this: Our sophomore-level college students consistently catch on to grammatical diagramming after just three to four weeks of practice. The move to semantic diagramming comes after students are accomplished at grammatical diagramming. Our students have found diagramming to be among the most productive aspects of the entire exegetical process.

In a typical week in second-year Greek, we give assignments ahead of time and students come to class ready to discuss their conclusions. For a three-hour course that meets three times a week, we use Monday and Wednesday to parse and translate the assigned text and to identify the syntax of the assigned terms. On Friday we have our weekly vocabulary quiz, discuss the students' diagrams of the passage, and wrap up our discussion of that particular text.

Advanced Greek

At the advanced level (typically the third year), students are introduced to a twelve-step method of exegesis and exposition that takes them from the biblical text to personal application, then on to a teaching or preaching outline. You may want to introduce students to the exegetical method sometime during their second year.

1— Spiritual Preparation
2— General Introduction
3— Literary Context
4— Provisional Translation
5— Grammatical Diagram
6— Semantic Diagram and Provisional Outline
7— Word and Concept Analysis
8— Broader Biblical and Theological Contexts
9— Commentaries and Special Studies
10— Polished Translation and Extended Paraphrase
11— Application
12— Preaching/Teaching Outline

Students take approximately fifteen verses through the entire method every two weeks. You could continue with the remaining passages in Mounce's *Graded Reader* or work in another part of the New Testament. It's entirely up to you. A typical two-week period in advanced Greek might follow this schedule:

Week 1:		Week 2:	
Monday	— Steps 1–4	Monday	— Step 6
Wednesday	— Steps 1–4	Wednesday	— Steps 7–10
Friday	— Step 5	Friday	— Steps 11–12

SOME ADVANTAGES OF THIS APPROACH

We see at least five pedagogical advantages to the approach developed in *Biblical Greek Exegesis*. (1) Students move from the New Testament to the Greek grammars, a direction that keeps interest high and offers a contextual check on the learning process. (2) The graded approach introduces students to the easier passages first. This builds their confidence and equips them to do the more difficult passages that follow. (3) Students learn to do grammatical and semantic diagramming in order to understand the larger units. Recent advances in applying linguistic theory to the study of the New Testament have shown that meaning is governed more by the larger units or discourses than by isolated words or phrases. (4) The approach gives students tools for working effectively in analyzing larger units of material. (4) The approach is holistic in that it integrates the study of Greek with the larger process of understanding and applying the message of the New Testament. (5) Students learn how to use the various exegetical tools by watching their teachers move (and sometimes struggle) through the process themselves.

HOW TO USE THIS BOOK IN TEACHING

In Intermediate and Advanced Greek Courses

Biblical Greek Exegesis may be used in upper-level Greek courses in a variety of ways. Our plan looks something like this. As we mentioned earlier, our **first-year students** use Mounce's *Basics of Biblical Greek* (textbook and workbook). We require that our **second-year students** use *Biblical Greek Exegesis* in combination with Mounce's *Graded Reader* and a vocabulary guide.[5] Again, since the exercises in Section One of *Biblical Greek Exegesis* are based on the passages in the first half of Mounce's *Graded Reader*, teachers have syntax and diagramming exercises for nine major sections of the New Testament, plenty for most intermediate Greek courses. About midway through the second year we recommend that students who have not already done so purchase a standard lexicon and reference grammar.[6] Our **third-year students** advance to Section Two of our workbook, where they begin to take different texts through the entire exegetical process. You can also introduce students to the exegetical method in Section Two during their second year of study. In addition to the above resources we encourage our students to work through a primer on textual criticism.[7]

Our hope is that *Biblical Greek Exegesis* will prove to be a useful tool for helping students make the difficult transition from the end of first-year Greek to more advanced studies. To make this happen we see great value in working with larger blocks of text, but we also believe we should introduce students to a variety of writing styles and literary types. *Biblical Greek Exegesis* does both. Intermediate Greek students learn to work with paragraphs, but they also experience a variety of texts over the course of the year. Furthermore, the texts are graded so that students progress in their study from the easier to the more difficult material. Advanced Greek students are not just repeating what they learned in their second year, they are moving on to integrate the study of syntax into the larger enterprise of New Testament exegesis. This helps them make strong connections between the study of Greek and their life and ministry.

In Upper-Level New Testament Exegesis Courses

Along with using *Biblical Greek Exegesis* for intermediate or advanced Greek, there is a completely different scenario where our workbook might prove useful. When teaching an upper-level exegesis course on a book of the New Testament, teachers often call for a supplementary text to guide the student through the exegetical process. Section Two of our workbook presents a comprehensive exegetical method that can be applied to any book of New Testament. Students are given clear, step-by-step instructions along with examples from the New Testament and a select bibliography of resources.

---

5. We recommend Warren C. Trenchard's, *The Student's Complete Vocabulary Guide to the Greek New Testament* (Grand Rapids: Zondervan, 1992).

6. The standard lexicon is that of Walter Bauer, *A Greek-English Lexicon of the New Testament and Other Early Christian Literature*, ed. W. F. Arndt, F. W. Gingrich, F. W. Danker, 2d ed. (Chicago: Univ. of Chicago Press, 1979). On the topic of a grammar, we recommend Dan Wallace's *Greek Grammar Beyond the Basics* for a couple of reasons. First, our students are already familiar with his syntax terminology. Second, they can begin using Wallace as an intermediate grammar and gradually grow into the more technical discussions it affords. As Bruce Metzger says, Wallace's *Greek Grammar* is "a first-rate work." Here you have an intermediate grammar and reference grammar rolled into one. Other intermediate-level grammars worth noting include James A. Brooks and Carlton L. Winbery, *Syntax of New Testament Greek* (Lanham, Md.: Univ. Press of America, 1979), and Richard A. Young, *Intermediate New Testament Greek: A Linguistic and Exegetical Approach* (Nashville: Broadman and Holman, 1994).

7. One of the best is J. Harold Greenlee, *Introduction to New Testament Textual Criticism*, rev. ed. (Peabody, Mass: Hendrickson, 1995).

Preface for Students

WELCOME TO *BIBLICAL GREEK EXEGESIS*

Congratulations on completing your first year of Greek study! You have made it through what many consider to be the most difficult and least gratifying year. No one said that memorizing paradigms and parsing participles would be loads of fun. And now you know why. It's not! As teachers we realize how much time you have invested and how hard you have worked to finish the first year. For your discipline and endurance we say, "Congratulations" and "Thank you, Lord!"

Are you ready to go beyond the basics and learn how to use Greek as the significant ministry tool it is purported to be? (Please make sure you read the last part in this preface: "Why Study Greek in Preparation for Christian Ministry?") The aim of *Biblical Greek Exegesis* is to guide you through the intermediate and advanced stages of study. We developed this tool with one primary goal in mind: to equip you to use a comprehensive exegetical method to move from the pages of the Greek New Testament to application in the modern world. As you grow in your study of the New Testament, you will see that study transform your life and ministry. After all, these documents were written for life impact.

Biblical Greek Exegesis is organized into two main sections. **Section One** is meant to be used in connection with William Mounce's *Graded Reader*, a textbook that presents twenty New Testament Greek passages in graded order (i.e., progressing from the easier to the more difficult). *Biblical Greek Exegesis* offers syntax and diagramming exercises for the first nine passages in the *Graded Reader*. Whereas in beginning Greek you learned mainly about word patterns (morphology), much of intermediate Greek will be devoted to learning about how words relate to other words or sentence patterns (syntax). For advanced Greek we turn to **Section Two** in our workbook. Here we incorporate all you have learned about words and sentences into a twelve-step exegetical process that teaches you how to understand and apply the message of the Greek New Testament.

We want you to hear what some of our own students have to say about their experience with the approach used in *Biblical Greek Exegesis*. But before we share their stories, allow us to mention just a few ways you can benefit from our approach.

HOW CAN THE APPROACH USED IN THIS BOOK HELP YOU?

For starters, *Biblical Greek Exegesis* takes a *real-world approach* to learning intermediate and advanced Greek. You will learn by moving from the Greek New Testament to the grammars and other reference tools, the way you will do things in the "real world." This means that in the process you will develop habits of learning Greek that will prepare you to actually use Greek in life and ministry. Besides, we think you will find this approach much more enjoyable than most traditional approaches. (At some point you might be interested in reading "The Need for a New Approach" in the Preface for Teachers.)

As a related benefit, *Biblical Greek Exegesis* helps you *bridge the gap between studying Greek formally in the classroom and the larger enterprise of using Greek in your personal study and ministry*. We have seen too many people invest enormous amounts of time and energy in studying biblical Greek only to let it waste away when faced with the urgent demands of everyday ministry. That is understandable since it is difficult to see how a "hortatory subjunctive" or a "double accusative" can be connected in any meaningful way to a person with a terminal illness or a congregation facing a crucial decision. Perhaps as teachers we are guilty of assuming that once students know Greek, they automatically know how to use Greek in ministry. We want you as students to *learn how to integrate your knowledge of Greek into a comprehensive interpretive process* that equips you to draw an accurate yet applicable message from the pages of the New Testament. *Biblical Greek Exegesis* is more than a refresher course or a summary of Greek essentials. We have designed it to help you make connections between the solutions found in the Greek text and the needs and problems of people.

There is at least one other way our approach can help you. In using *Biblical Greek Exegesis* you will *learn to do more than study words and analyze syntax.* All too often pastors and teachers have been trained only to work with smaller units (words, phrases, clauses, and even sentences) to the neglect of larger units (paragraphs and discourses). Yet linguists insist on the priority of context for determining meaning. If we want to understand the meaning of a text, we must have tools crafted especially for working with a text at a number of different contextual levels (pictured in the "language ladder" below).[1]

| Discourses |
| Paragraphs |
| Sentences |
| Clauses |
| Phrases |
| Words |
| Parts of Words |
| Sounds |

In *Biblical Greek Exegesis* you will learn how to discover the meaning of the text at the paragraph and discourse levels, where topics and themes are most fully developed.

WHAT ARE OUR STUDENTS SAYING?

We have been using the approach embodied in *Biblical Greek Exegesis* at both the intermediate and advanced levels of Greek pedagogy for several years. Our programs have increased numerically, and student motivation has risen as they are engaged in serious Bible study using the Greek text. The experience has been rewarding, especially because we have the privilege of working with outstanding students. We thought you might like to hear from some of them.

"Working through translations for the purpose of developing a solid understanding of Greek syntax, as well as learning how to grammatically and semantically diagram passages, lays a firm foundation upon which sound exegesis can be built. Utilizing these skills in the interpretation of major blocks of text with the twelve-step exegetical method was the climax of my undergraduate career. This method not only teaches valuable lessons in proper exegesis, it makes the process of learning this information fun."

Jonathan Davis, seminary student, Union 97 graduate

"New Testament Greek has been the type of class I've always dreamed of, but never had. My whole purpose in coming to college was to be in an environment where I could be challenged not only to make a good grade but also to learn. This class not only pumped my mind full of information but also taught me how to discover for myself and motivated me to do so."

Chad Pollock, seminary student, OBU 96 graduate

---

1. For a recent overview of discourse analysis and its value for New Testament studies, see chapter 21 on "Discourse Analysis" in Stanley E. Porter, *Idioms of the Greek New Testament* (Sheffield: Sheffield Academic Press, 1992). For more on the various levels in language, see the chapter entitled "Introducing Linguistics" in David Alan Black, *Linguistics for Students of New Testament Greek: A Survey of Basic Concepts and Applications*, 2d ed. (Grand Rapids: Baker, 1995), and the first two chapters ("From Words to Paragraphs" and "The Greek Paragraph") in Kendell H. Easley, *User-Friendly Greek: A Common Sense Approach to the Greek New Testament* (Nashville: Broadman and Holman, 1994).

"Semantic diagramming has served as the culmination of my entire Greek and hermeneutical education. Simple translation does not provide the "bridge" needed to effectively integrate Greek into interpretation and ministry. This model has shown me how useful Greek can be in my own ministry."

Klay Aspinwall, seminary student, Union 96 graduate

"I believe New Testament Greek is the best class I have ever taken. This class taught me how to use everything I learned in first-year Greek. Without this class, I probably would have never really worked with Greek again."

Kim Baker, graduate student, OBU 96 graduate

"Without a doubt, Dr. Guthrie's Biblical Greek Exegesis course was the most rewarding course I attended at Union University. It prepared me for graduate work and laid a solid foundation for a lifetime of enriching Bible study. My appreciation for the New Testament Scriptures exploded, my personal devotional life was challenged, and I was taught how to responsibly handle the Greek text. I consider it a great blessing to have attended Dr. Guthrie's course."

William Myatt, seminary student, Union 97 graduate

"The new exegetical method has been an invaluable tool in my study of Greek. The basic yet comprehensive method not only aids me in my understanding of Greek today, but is also preparing and equipping me to teach in the future. Anyone who is dedicated to the understanding and applying the Greek text will greatly benefit from this method."

Brooke Worrell, Union student

"Coming into New Testament Greek, I had one goal: I wanted to learn how to put into practice all of the things I learned in my first two semesters of Greek. I didn't want to leave with just a bunch of rules of grammar and a limited vocabulary. I wanted to learn a method that would make all of the stuff worthwhile. This class met that expectation and so much more."

Chantal Bunn, OBU 96 graduate

"Proper interpretation is based on solid and detailed exegesis. This step-by-step process allows the interpreter to make appropriate and applicable interpretations. After grappling with the text in this way, the text comes alive, and the importance of precise exegesis is seen. Learning this exegetical process has better prepared me to follow Christ and to communicate his word."

Jason Dukes, seminary student, Union 97 graduate

"I can honestly say that this was the best class I have had at OBU."

Drew Smith, seminary student, OBU 94 graduate

"Since I desire the skills for proper interpretation of Scripture, I am indebted to the exegetical method for its step-by-step help. I now feel confident in my ability to handle God's word effectively. Not only has the method been instrumental in my growth in interpretation, it has also challenged me to glean contemporary application from the Scriptures. This method will play a vital role in my life. . . ."

Dax Hughes, seminary student, Union 97 graduate

"After taking this class, I can honestly say that I have been given a very effective tool that will help me communicate the truth of God's Word to a world starving for relevant truth."

Joey Dodson, seminary student, OBU 97 graduate

"I feel very equipped now, not only with an understanding of the diagramming method, but also with an understanding of textual criticism. Also I feel as if I have been thoroughly exposed to the resources I will need to continue practicing this method on my own."

Rix White, graduate student, OBU 97 graduate

"The method of Greek presented by Drs. Guthrie and Duvall is organized and clear. This method is helpful in that the student benefits from the teacher's expertise but also learns skills for personal study. This is an exciting means of learning; it is exciting to be translating passages and "digging" through the meaning as one learns. Although I know no other way of learning Greek syntax and diagramming, I see no need to. This method provides a valuable means of learning, resulting in a great sense of accomplishment."

Kelly Swain, Union student

"This class has furthered my knowledge of Greek, my walk with the Lord (the purpose of studying Greek), my discipline and responsibility as a student, and my preparation for the Christian ministry."

Justin Hardin, seminary student, OBU 97 graduate

"The way in which we have approached studying Greek during this second year has helped to bring back some of the excitement of studying biblical Greek. The enthusiasm that was lost while trying to hammer down basics of grammar in the first year has been rediscovered as I learn how to do exegesis. The translation assignments are in an easy format to understand, and the diagramming exercises are challenging and fun. My personal Bible studies have matured as I realize the importance of not only reading the surface of the Scriptures, but also dwelling on the word meanings and the context in order to communicate the Word of God."

John Whiteside, Union student

"In New Testament Greek we combined the nuts and bolts of syntax and semantics with desire to be relevant to today's audience. We learned the tools to use the language without divorcing this from the reason we were learning the language: Greek exegesis."

Ben Blackwell, OBU 97 graduate

WHY STUDY GREEK AS A PART OF CHRISTIAN LIFE AND MINISTRY?

As you can see, our students are highly motivated because they see the study of Greek as a significant part of their lives. We all need a meaningful answer to the question, "Why am I studying Greek anyway?" because we need a "why" (the underlying reason) to sustain the "what" (the daily discipline of learning). After you read our brief rationale for studying Greek in preparation for Christian life and ministry, we encourage you to write out your own.[2]

1.   We were made for God and need God.

In the opening chapter of the Bible we read: "So God created man in his own image, in the image of God he created him; male and female he created them" (Gen. 1:27). Whatever else this theologically loaded phrase "image of God" may mean, it certainly declares that we are relational beings who were made for God and need God. Evangelical theologian Alister McGrath explains:

We are made in the image of God. We have an inbuilt capacity—indeed, an inbuilt *need*—to relate to God. Nothing that is transitory can ever fill this need. To fail to relate to God is to fail to be completely human. To be fulfilled is to be filled by God. Nothing that is not God can ever hope to take the place of God.[3]

In this context the famous words in the prayer of the early church leader Augustine of Hippo ring true: "You [God] have made us for yourself, and our hearts are restless until they rest in you."[4] The rationale for studying Greek ultimately must relate to one's relationship with God. You should study and apply the Greek New Testament as an act of devotion to your Creator.

You may be one of those students who is motivated to study biblical Greek simply because you love to learn new things, including languages. When it comes to languages, you have an insatiable curiosity to discover how those tiny threads we call words have been woven into a literary tapestry. For you, New Testament Greek is a thing of beauty and studying Greek an adventure or an act of

---

2. You might also enjoy reading the opening chapters in the older work by A. T. Robertson, "The Minister's Use of His Greek New Testament," in *The Minister and His Greek New Testament* (repr. Grand Rapids: Baker, 1977), and the more recent work by David Alan Black, "You and Your Greek New Testament: Clarifying Objectives," in *Using New Testament Greek in Ministry: A Practical Guide for Students and Pastors* (Grand Rapids: Baker, 1993).

3. Alister E. McGrath, *Intellectuals Don't Need God and Other Modern Myths* (Grand Rapids: Zondervan, 1993), 30.

4. Augustine, *Confessions*, 1.1.1. trans. Henry Chadwick. (Oxford: Oxford Univ. Press, 1991), 3.

worship. If this is your motivation, we believe it too stems from your being made in the image of God. We are driven to discover and are able to appreciate the beauty inherent in language precisely because we have been created in our Creator's likeness.

2. God has revealed himself to us.

So that we can come to know him, God has taken the initiative to reach out to us. He has revealed himself or made himself known through his actions and his words, and, supremely, through his Son Jesus Christ. The writer to the Hebrews begins his sermon by noting, "In the past God spoke to our forefathers through the prophets at many times and in various ways, but in these last days he has spoken to us by his Son" (Heb. 1:1–2).

3. Scripture is the inspired written record of God's special revelation.

In Paul's final charge to his faithful friend and coworker Timothy, he announces that "all Scripture is God-breathed" (2 Tim. 3:16). The term "God-breathed" (NIV) or "inspired" (NRSV) indicates that Scripture—the written record of God's revelation—has been breathed out of the mouth of God; that is, it is God's speech or word. Millard Erickson explains: "By inspiration of Scripture we mean that supernatural influence of the Holy Spirit upon the Scripture writers which rendered their writings an accurate record of the revelation."[5]

4. In Scripture, God speaks of divine solutions to basic human problems and needs.

In this inspired written record we read of solutions to our needs and problems, beginning with our most basic of problems—the sin problem. From the same passage in 2 Timothy 3, Paul says Scripture makes us "wise for salvation through faith in Christ Jesus" (3:15) and proves useful for "teaching, rebuking, correcting, and training in righteousness" (3:16b). In other words, Scripture offers good news of a God-sent Savior (the solution to our most basic problem) as well as guidance in Christian belief (doctrine) and behavior (ethics).

5. God calls us to a life of study toward a deeper understanding of Scripture for both personal edification and ministry to others.

As our understanding of Scripture deepens, its potential impact on our lives and ministries increases. To be sure, we can understand without applying, but how can we apply what we do not understand? Some may object: Why is it necessary that we work hard to study the text well? Isn't it clear enough for anyone to understand? Do we really need to go to the trouble of learning the original languages?

Certainly the central message of Scripture is plain. And yes, the Holy Spirit is our Teacher (John 14:26; 16:13). But not everything in Scripture is easy to understand. Even one apostle (Peter) admitted that another apostle's letters (Paul's) "contain some things that are hard to understand" (2 Peter 3:16). From our vantage point, certain things in Scripture are hard to comprehend because of the gap between our world and the biblical world. In many instances—because of vast differences in time and culture (e.g., the difference in language)—we need to build bridges to allow people in our world (ourselves included) to understand and apply the message spoken in the biblical world.[6] God wants us to study diligently to come to a deeper understanding of his Word in order that we may apply its message more effectively.

---

5. Millard J. Erickson, *Christian Theology* (Grand Rapids: Baker, 1983), 199.

6. In *How to Read the Bible for All Its Worth: A Guide to Understanding the Bible*, 2d ed. (Grand Rapids: Zondervan, 1993), 17, Gordon D. Fee and Douglas Stuart summarize the necessity of interpretation: "Because the Bible is *God's Word*, it has *eternal relevance*; it speaks to all humankind, in every age and in every culture. Because it is God's Word, we must listen—and obey. But because God chose to speak his Word through *human words in history*, every book in the Bible also has *historical particularity*; each document is conditioned by the language, time, and culture in which it was originally written. . . . Interpretation of the Bible is demanded by the 'tension' that exists between its *eternal relevance* and its *historical particularity*."

6. **The sharper our interpretive tools, the deeper our understanding of the text of Scripture and, consequently, the greater the impact on our lives and ministries.**

If you happened to have used Bill Mounce's first-year Greek grammar, you may remember his little illustration about overhauling a car engine.

> What tools will you select? I would surmise that with a screw driver, hammer, a pair of pliers, and perhaps a crow bar, you could make some progress. But look at the chances you are taking. Without a socket wrench you could ruin many of the bolts. Without a torque wrench you cannot get the head seated properly. The point is, without the proper tools you run the risk of doing a minimal job, and perhaps actually hurting the engine.[7]

God can use anyone, but all other things being equal, he will often choose to use the better-equipped and more adequately trained human instrument to accomplish his purpose. What complicates matters is that "all other things" are many times not equal. A person with a sharp mind may not have a pure heart, or a person obviously gifted in teaching may not display the Spirit's fruit of self-control or love. Someone possessing a profound grasp of biblical Greek may be living in blatant rebellion, while God may be working powerfully through a person who doesn't know the first letter of the Greek alphabet. But are we limited to an either-or choice here? As we prepare for life and ministry, must we settle for *either* developing a keen mind *or* cultivating a clean heart? Should we be forced to choose between the head and the heart, between understanding and passion? Jesus' greatest commandment clearly calls for a both-and kind of love for God (Matt. 22:37–38). We need a loyalty that resists compartmentalization and a deep devotion to God that involves every aspect of our being.

If you decide to take a both-and approach to Christian life and ministry, knowledge of biblical Greek constitutes one of the most significant interpretive tools you can acquire, and certainly one worth sharpening. Think, for instance, about some of the things you will be able to do if you know Greek:

- understand the original text for personal renewal and application;
- understand and evaluate modern translations, commentaries, and sermons;
- gain additional insights for use in service to Christ and the church (e.g., through counseling)
- teach God's Word with confidence, knowing that you are faithfully communicating what God has said;
- discern the difference between true and false doctrine and contend for the faith.

IN SUMMARY

As you sharpen your Greek tools, your understanding of Scripture will deepen. As your understanding deepens, so should your ability to build bridges between the scriptural message and the modern audience (provided you also read the modern audience carefully). In building bridges you will fulfill your call to explain and apply God's message to people's lives, including your own. And as people appropriate God's Word in their lives, they will experience the purpose for which God created them—to know and love and glorify him. The bottom line, then, is that we learn Greek as a means of doing a better job of loving God and our neighbor (Matt. 22:37–40).

In conclusion, we offer the following dictum printed in the Latin Preface to Johannes Albrecht Bengel's 1734 edition of the Greek New Testament: **"Apply yourself totally to the text; apply the text totally to yourself."**[8] It is hard to imagine a more appropriate aim for a person preparing for Christian ministry.

---

7. Mounce, *Basics of Biblical Greek*, 3.

8. Cited by Bruce M. Metzger in the Foreword to John R. Kohlenberger, III, *The Greek New Testament: UBS4 with NRSV and NIV* (Grand Rapids: Zondervan, 1993).

Section One

A Graded Approach to Learning Biblical Greek Syntax

Introduction

In this first section of *Biblical Greek Exegesis*, "A Graded Approach to Learning Biblical Greek Syntax," we provide syntax and diagramming exercises for the following New Testament passages (the first nine in Mounce's *Graded Reader*): 1 John 1:1–2:2; 2:28–3:10; John 15:1–27; Mark 1:1–28; Mark 8:27–9:8; Colossians 1:1–23; Matthew 6:5–34; Romans 3:21–26; 5:1–11; 8:1–17; James 1:1–21; and Philippians 1:27–2:13. You will be working with large blocks of text from different New Testament literary types, divided into smaller units of about four to seven verses. During a typical week you will be asked to parse and translate the text, identify the syntax of selected terms, and diagram a smaller segment of the passage. Read on to find out more about the syntax exercises, the diagramming methods, and the vocabulary assignment.

WHAT TO EXPECT FROM THE SYNTAX EXERCISES

When we study *syntax*, we are trying to understand how words function within a sentence. In your first year of study you learned how to identify the form of a particular word (e.g., a noun in the nominative case). The next step is to discover how that word relates to other words in the immediate context. In the expression from Mark 2:28 below, there are two words that are nominative in form: "lord" (κύριος) and "son" (υἱὸς). That much you already know.

Mark 2:28 κύριός ἐστιν ὁ υἱὸς τοῦ ἀνθρώπου καὶ τοῦ σαββάτου.
The Son of man is Lord even of the Sabbath.

When we analyze the syntax of these two nouns in the nominative case, we are trying to discover how they relate to other words in the sentence. The expression ὁ υἱὸς is said to be a *subject* nominative whereas κύριος is a *predicate* nominative. Even though they are both nominative in form, we use the terms "subject" and "predicate" (often referred to as syntax categories) to describe the distinct role each word plays in the sentence.

You will begin your study of syntax with the exercise from 1 John 1:1–4:

1. ἑωράκαμεν (1)   (tense) _____
2. ὀφθαλμοῖς (1)   <u>Instrumental dative of means</u>
3. ζωῆς (1)   (case) _____
4. ζωὴ (2)   (case) _____
5. ὑμῖν (2)   (case) _____
6. second καὶ (3)   (function) _____
7. κοινωνίαν (3)   (case) _____
8. ἣ πεπληρωμένη (4)   (construction) _____

After each term the verse number appears in parenthesis. Beside the answer blank we offer a clarifying "clue" to help you know what to look for when identifying the syntax of the Greek word. For example, you are to identify the syntax of the first term ἑωράκαμεν with respect to "tense" and the syntax of the third term ζωῆς with respect to "case." We only use about six such "clues": tense, voice, mood, case, function, and construction. The "construction" clue is used when two elements work together to play a role in the sentence (conditional clauses or periphrastic constructions). We use the "function" clue for just about everything that does not fit neatly into one of the others (e.g., the function of definite articles, participles, infinitives, conjunctions).

You will notice that we have supplied the answer for the second word. The term ὀφθαλμοῖς from 1 John 1:1 is an instrumental dative of means. Actually we cannot take credit for giving away the answer. When we provide an answer (highlighted by underlining), we are incorporating an insight found in the "Exegetical Discussion" section of Mounce's *Graded Reader*. Since many of you will be using both books, we thought you might find this feature helpful.

How do we use these syntax exercises in the classroom? We typically tell our students, "In addition to translating and diagramming, you are responsible for identifying the syntax of the assigned terms. After parsing each term, go to the syntax summary (see the discussion below), see the possibilities, then come back and tell the class how you think each term functions syntactically in its context." The strategy here is to get you to work inductively from the New Testament back to a consideration of the syntax categories, the way you will approach the Greek text in the real world. During the class period for which the assignment is performed, you will share your answers to the exercises. Our job as teachers is to clarify the syntax categories in question and guide you through the interpretive process. Periodically we review the syntax categories learned thus far and fill in the gaps by introducing the few categories not covered in the assigned passages.

Let us explain what we mean by *syntax summary* so that you are not confused by the terminology. There are two different syntax summaries that students need to be concerned with.

1. The syntax summary in Dan Wallace's **Greek Grammar Beyond the Basics**

When we tell you to go to the "syntax summary" and see the possibilities, we are talking about this summary of syntax categories. We suggest that you begin with the partial summary on pp. 141–82 of Mounce's *Graded Reader* and eventually move to the full summary on pp. 726–69 of Wallace's *Greek Grammar*. We find these summaries advantageous because they are linked to an advanced grammar and we like to see our students moving in that direction.

2. A student's syntax summary

Because most of us learn better by participating rather than spectating, we ask our students to build their own syntax summary complete with definitions and examples coming out of their study of the Greek New Testament. We provide a basic outline called a "student's syntax summary" (see the appendix) to get them started and keep them organized. Over the course of the year they fill in the outline. The practice of writing down a definition and citing examples from their own study reinforces their understanding of the syntax categories. At the end of the year we ask them to turn in a typed syntax notebook. They love us for it!

Tip: An alternative approach is to have the students use a highlighter to mark or highlight the syntax categories in Mounce or Wallace's syntax summary as those categories are covered in class. That way they can flip through the summary and see immediately the categories already covered.

Throughout the process of using the Wallace summary and building your own, you are focusing on the text of the New Testament; that is what keeps interest running high.

A WORD ABOUT DIAGRAMMING

Part of your weekly assignment will include diagramming. Even the mention of the word *diagramming* may strike fear in your heart. As we say more about this valuable tool, please remember three important things. (1) You will begin with short, simple diagramming exercises and gradually build your diagramming skills. There will be time to learn the skill. (2) As is to be expected with any new method, learning grammatical and semantic diagramming will take some time, but don't let it overwhelm you. Our diagramming methods may look complex at first glance, but our sophomore-level college students consistently catch on after just three to four weeks of practice, and you can too. After this initial learning curve, we predict that you will get excited about the approach because you will begin to see that there is nothing quite like diagramming for helping you grasp the meaning of a passage. (3) Most methods of diagramming require a degree of personalization in matters of detail (e.g., the extent to which you subdivide a phrase, whether or not to use lines and arrows to clarify relationships, and so on). We encourage you to embrace the basic approach and modify it in ways that make it useful to you.

We use two types of diagramming. Grammatical and semantic diagramming combine to help you analyze the linguistic structure of a text—perhaps the single most significant step in the exegetical process. To understand and clarify the syntactical relationships within sentences we use *grammatical* diagramming. But there are other important relationships within a text that cannot be seen with grammatical diagramming alone. We also need to grasp how an author's argument flows through a passage. Our tool for seeing how sentences relate to other sentences and how paragraphs relate to other paragraphs is *semantic* diagramming. You will begin by doing only grammatical diagramming. The move to semantic diagramming comes after you are accomplished at grammatical diagramming. Our students have found grammatical and semantic diagramming to be one of the most exciting aspects of the exegetical process.

Our approach to mapping the structure of a text furnishes a single tool that is powerful because of its flexibility.[1] If you wish to show specific grammatical relationships between many of the smaller units in a text, you may do so with precision. If, on the other hand, you are primarily interested in tracing an author's overall argument at the paragraph level and beyond, you may do that as well. Grammatical and semantic diagramming are designed to work together, with the former serving as the foundation for the latter. Most important of all, diagramming forces us to make decisions about how words and phrases work together in a text to communicate certain messages. In the sections that follow, we will explain in detail how to do both types of diagramming, using passages from Colossians as examples.

VOCABULARY, VOCABULARY, VOCABULARY

If you are still reading this Introduction, you must have made it through the section on diagramming. We're impressed! If we were to launch into a long lecture on learning vocabulary, we would risk losing you, so we have decided to push this one off on your teacher. Your teacher will make the vocabulary assignment in each exercise. Some teachers prefer to have you review the words you learned during your first year, while others will want you to push ahead and learn new words. For your convenience you might want to obtain one of the recent vocabulary guides.[2]

---

1. Our method is a modification of the block diagramming method developed by our professor at Southwestern Baptist Theological Seminary, Lorin L. Cranford. See his *Study Manual of The Epistle of James: English Text* (Fort Worth: AlphaGraphics, 1987). There are a variety of tools available to the interpreter for analyzing these kinds of relationships, including word-by-word line diagramming (Brooks and Winbery, *Syntax of New Testament Greek*, 154–63), colon analysis (Louw, *Semantics of New Testament Greek*, 91–158), sentence-flow diagramming (Fee, *New Testament Exegesis*, 65–80), thought-flow diagramming (Young, *Intermediate New Testament Greek*, 267–77), paragraph-flow diagramming (Easley, *User-Friendly Greek*, 19–34), and phrasing (Mounce, *Graded Reader*, xv–xxiii).

2. We recommend to our students the book by Warren C. Trenchard, *The Student's Complete Vocabulary Guide to the Greek New Testament* (Grand Rapids: Zondervan, 1992). See also Thomas A. Robinson, *Mastering Greek Vocabulary* (Peabody, Mass.: Hendrickson, 1990), and Robert E. Van Voorst, *Building Your New Testament Greek Vocabulary* (Grand Rapids: Eerdmans, 1990).

How to Do
Grammatical Diagramming

Grammatical diagramming serves as our primary tool for clarifying the relationships between words and groups of words in a biblical text. In this section we will spell out the basic principles of grammatical diagramming and illustrate the method using Colossians 3:1-4.[3] The "Grammatical Diagramming Paradigm" below offers a one-page reference tool on how to do grammatical diagramming.

Although grammatical diagramming may look complicated at first, notice that there are *fewer than ten "positions" to learn.* Once you have learned these very simple rules for placing various parts of a sentence, the *method* of diagramming becomes easy. On the other hand, discerning the roles different parts of a Greek sentence play can be challenging; but that is a task you must undertake to interpret any passage, whether you use our diagramming method or not. As you develop your skill, you will find the art of grammatical diagramming aiding you in discerning the function of parts of the sentence. Consequently, diagramming becomes an indispensable tool for moving from an analysis of the text to a teaching/preaching outline.

We and our students have become convinced that grammatical and semantic diagramming offer vital, powerful help for communicating the text well and in line with accurate exegesis. In fact, many of our students tell us that diagramming is the most helpful aspect of the exegetical process. It may take you several weeks to get comfortable with this method, but those weeks will prove a worthy investment.

GRAMMATICAL DIAGRAMMING PARADIGM

General Instructions

- Symbols (. . . ^) are used to show original word order. Ellipsis points (. . .) mark the original location while the caret (^) is placed beside words that have been moved.
- In appositional situations we place one member directly above the other and mark the relationship using two vertical lines (| |).
- Grammatical parallels are shown using a single vertical line (e.g., the vertical line to the left of the objects below).
- Elliptical expressions are indicated by a series of dashes (-----).
- Vertical dotted lines are sometimes used to show the connection between modifiers and the elements they modify.
- Direct discourse is indented eight spaces and bracketed by vertically aligned dots (•).

---

3. You may be the kind of person who likes to see an example first and read the instructions later. If so, skip to "Colossians 3:1-4 as Example" and read through the section "Notes on the Diagram of Colossians 3:1–4," where we explain the diagram of these four verses in detail. (Your teacher may want to work through this example with you.)

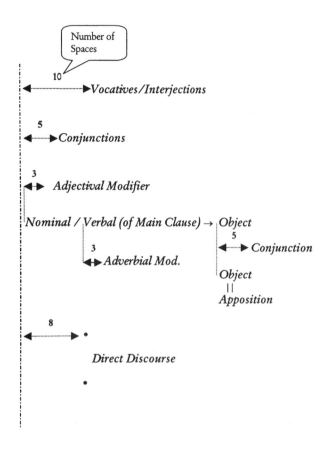

BASIC PRINCIPLES OF GRAMMATICAL DIAGRAMMING

1. All main clauses begin on the far left margin and are kept on the same line.

Write the verse reference to the left of the main clause (perhaps in bold superscript). We have found it useful to add letters to the verse reference when there is more than one main clause in a single verse, as in James 1:11a and 1:11b:

γὰρ

1.11a   ἀνέτειλεν ὁ ἥλιος

σὺν τῷ καύσωνι

καὶ

1.11b   ἐξήρανεν → τὸν χόρτον,

2. The sequential order of each Greek sentence is followed for the most part.

Preserving the sequential order of the Greek sentence makes it easier to see the author's flow of thought as well as the unit's linguistic structure. Since an attempt is made to maintain the original order, when modifiers occur before the element they modify, we diagram them on the line above. When modifiers come after what they modify, we diagram them on the line below. You can see both situations in the diagram of Romans 8:3b below (note the position of both prepositional phrases):

καὶ

περὶ ἁμαρτίας

8.3b   κατέκρινεν → τὴν ἁμαρτίαν

ἐν τῇ σαρκί,

There are a few modifications to the rule of maintaining the word order of the Greek sentence.

- When words need to be removed from their original slot in order to show a grammatical relationship, ellipsis points (. . .) are used to mark the original location while the caret (^) precedes the element that has been moved. In Colossians 3:2a below the object ^τὰ ἄνω originally preceded the verb φρονεῖτε.

3.2a ... φρονεῖτε → ^τὰ ἄνω,

As a general rule we encourage you to read the diagram from top to bottom until you reach the main clause, then read from left to right. See the "Notes on the Diagram of Colossians 3:1–4," below, for more explanation.

- We move postpositive conjunctions (such as γὰρ in Heb. 4:15a below) to the beginning of the sentence and indent them five spaces from the left margin. Vocatives and interjections (such as Ἰδοὺ in Mark 1:2b below) are moved to the beginning of the sentence and indented ten spaces. We do not use the symbols . . . ^ for postpositive terms.

γὰρ
4:15a οὐ ἔχομεν → ἀρχιερέα

Ἰδοὺ
1.2b ἀποστέλλω → τὸν ἄγγελόν

- We move direct and indirect objects to the right of the verb and signal such objects by an arrow (see Mark 1:2b above). Two arrows might be needed in the case of double accusatives, as with the first part of Mark 8:31 below.

Καὶ
8.31 ἤρξατο διδάσκειν → αὐτοὺς
→ ὅτι δεῖ τὸν υἱὸν τοῦ ἀνθρώπου ... παθεῖν → ^πολλὰ

In a relative clause, when a relative pronoun also functions as the object of the verb (e.g., the ὃν in John 15:3 below), we have not pulled it out to the right as usual. On diagramming an indirect object within an object clause, see John 15:14 below.

ἤδη
15.3 ὑμεῖς καθαροί ἐστε
διὰ τὸν λόγον
ὃν λελάληκα →ὑμῖν·

15.14 ὑμεῖς φίλοι ... ἐστε
^μού
ἐὰν ποιῆτε → ἃ ἐγὼ ἐντέλλομαι → ὑμῖν.

You might not like the idea of disturbing word order just to highlight an object or you might prefer to highlight objects in some other manner. Either way, here is a case where you may want to personalize the method to suit your linguistic preferences.

3. Grammatical relationships are shown by indention.

Indent all vocative case forms and interjections **ten spaces** from the far left margin, as in the first part of Mark 1.2b below:

$$\text{Ἰδοὺ}$$

1.2b　　ἀποστέλλω → τὸν ἄγγελόν

We indent direct discourse **eight spaces** from the far left margin and bracket it by vertically aligned dots. This enables you to make a clear distinction between the narrative and the direct discourse (see Mark 8:34 below).

```
              Καὶ
         προσκαλεσάμενος → τὸν ὄχλον
                              σὺν τοῖς μαθηταῖς
         |                        αὐτοῦ
         |
  8.34   εἶπεν→ αὐτοῖς,

              •              ^ὀπίσω μου
                   Εἴ τις θέλει … ἀκολουθεῖν,
                ἀπαρνησάσθω → ἑαυτὸν

                      καὶ
                   ἀράτω → τὸν σταυρὸν
                              αὐτοῦ

                      καὶ
                   ἀκολουθείτω →μοι.
              •
```

Indent all coordinate conjunctions that link together main clauses **five spaces** from the far left margin (notice the γὰρ and καὶ in Col. 3:3 below).

```
              γὰρ
  3.3a    ἀπεθάνετε


              καὶ
  3.3b    ἡ ζωὴ    …    κέκρυπται
          ^ὑμῶν
                      | σὺν τῷ Χριστῷ
                      | ἐν τῷ θεῷ·
```

When coordinate conjunctions join subordinate expressions, the conjunctions are indented five spaces from the beginning margin established by the subordinate expressions, as with ἀλλὰ in Romans 8:9a below.

```
              δὲ
  8.9a    ὑμεῖς οὐκ ἐστὲ
                      | ἐν σαρκὶ
                      |     ἀλλὰ
                      | ἐν πνεύματι,
```

We indent all modifying elements—including words, phrases, and clauses serving either an adjectival or adverbial purpose—**three spaces** to the right of the first letter of the word they modify. Taking another look at Colossians 3:3, you will notice that the prepositional phrases σὺν τῷ Χριστῷ and ἐν τῷ θεῷ are indented three spaces to the right of the first letter of the verb κέκρυπται.

γὰρ
3.3a ἀπεθάνετε

καὶ
3.3b ἡ ζωὴ   ...   κέκρυπται
       ^ὑμῶν

                σὺν τῷ Χριστῷ
                ἐν τῷ θεῷ·

Sometimes we like to use dotted vertical lines to clarify subordinate expressions that are separated from the word they modify by several lines, as in John 15:24:

εἰ ... μὴ ἐποίησα → ^τὰ ἔργα
                   ἐν αὐτοῖς
                              ἃ οὐδεὶς ἄλλος ἐποίησεν,

15.24 οὐκ εἴχοσαν → ἁμαρτίαν

If subordinating elements end up on the same line, then continue spacing to the right to prevent confusion (see Rom. 8:7a below).

διότι
8.7a τὸ φρόνημα . . . . ἔχθρα,
      ^τῆς σαρκὸς   εἰς θεόν,

Modifications to the rules of indention include the following:
- If the word being modified has a definite article, the three spaces are counted from the first letter of the word itself, not from the article, as in 1 John 1:2b:

1.2b ἀπαγγέλλομεν → ὑμῖν τὴν ζωὴν
                        τὴν αἰώνιον

- Periphrastics and complementary infinitives are left on the same line as the preceding verbal, as in the first part of Mark 8:31:

Καὶ
8.31 ἤρξατο διδάσκειν → αὐτοὺς

- Some single-word modifiers may be best left on the main clause line, as with ὑμῶν in Colossians 3:3b below. You have to decide whether moving smaller units clarifies or confuses your understanding of the syntax of the text.

καὶ

3.3b ἡ ζωὴ . . . κέκρυπται

^ὑμῶν

or

καὶ

3.3b ἡ ζωὴ ὑμῶν κέκρυπται

- Some adjectival modifiers are best left with the word(s) they modify. For example, in the titular expression "the Son of Man" in Mark 8:31, we think it best not to indent "of Man" three spaces under and to the right of "Son," but to leave these words together on the same line since they function as a unit (cf. also the expression τῆς ἁμαρτίας καὶ τοῦ θανάτου in Rom. 8:2).
- When a modifier seems to modify an entire clause rather than a single word, we indent three spaces from the left margin established by the clause being modified (see the ὅταν in Col. 3:4 for a possible example).
- Predicate nominatives are left on the same line with the subject and linking verb, as in John 15:1a:

15.1a   Ἐγώ εἰμι ἡ ἄμπελος

- Appositional elements are placed directly under the word they rename, and this relationship is shown by two vertical lines (| |), as with Χριστὸς and ἡ ζωὴ in Colossians 3:4 below:

ὅταν ὁ Χριστὸς φανερωθῇ,

| |

ἡ ζωὴ ὑμῶν,

τότε

καὶ

3.4   ὑμεῖς ... φανερωθήσεσθε

^σὺν αὐτῷ

ἐν δόξῃ.

4. Other Instructions

- Skip a line between main clause statements when it helps to clarify the grammatical relationships (e.g., after some marks of punctuation and coordinating conjunctions). Notice that in 1 John 3:5 below we did not skip a line after the comma at ἐφανερώθη, but did skip one before the second καί. This spacing clarifies the place of the ἵνα clause. The rule of thumb is clarity.

$$
\begin{array}{l}
\qquad\qquad \text{καὶ} \\
\text{3.5} \quad \text{οἴδατε} \to \text{ὅτι} \ \Big|\ \text{ἐκεῖνος ἐφανερώθη,} \\
\qquad\qquad\qquad\qquad\qquad \text{ἵνα ... ἄρῃ} \to \text{ˆτὰς ἁμαρτίας} \\[2mm]
\qquad\qquad\qquad\qquad \text{καὶ} \\
\qquad\qquad\qquad\qquad\qquad \text{ˆἐν αὐτῷ} \\
\qquad\qquad\quad \text{ἁμαρτία ... οὐκ ἔστιν.}
\end{array}
$$

- Show parallel expressions by placing a vertical line to the left of the expressions. In 1 John 1:5a below, the two verbs following the relative pronoun ἣν are parallel. Therefore, we skip two spaces after the relative pronoun and draw the vertical line. The line serves as the left margin for the two verbs that follow.

$$
\begin{array}{l}
\qquad\qquad \text{Καὶ} \\
\text{1.5a} \quad \text{ἔστιν αὕτη ἡ ἀγγελία} \\
\qquad\qquad\quad \text{ἣν} \ \Big|\ \text{ἀκηκόαμεν} \\
\qquad\qquad\qquad\qquad \text{ἀπ᾽ αὐτοῦ} \\[2mm]
\qquad\qquad\qquad\qquad \text{καὶ} \\
\qquad\qquad\qquad \text{ἀναγγέλλομεν} \to \text{ὑμῖν}
\end{array}
$$

Sometimes, however, elements that are indented the same number of spaces are not necessarily parallel. In Mark 1:14–15a below, κηρύσσων and λέγων are parallel, but neither seems parallel with the preceding prepositional phrase εἰς τὴν Γαλιλαίαν.

$$
\begin{array}{l}
\qquad\qquad \text{δὲ} \\
\qquad\qquad \text{Μετὰ τὸ παραδοθῆναι τὸν Ἰωάννην} \\
\text{1.14} \quad \text{ἦλθεν ὁ Ἰησοῦς} \\
\qquad\qquad \text{εἰς τὴν Γαλιλαίαν} \\
\qquad\qquad \text{κηρύσσων} \to \text{τὸ εὐαγγέλιον} \\
\qquad\qquad\qquad\qquad\qquad \text{τοῦ θεοῦ} \\[2mm]
\text{1.15} \qquad\quad \text{καὶ} \\
\qquad\qquad \text{λέγων} \to \text{ὅτι Πεπλήρωται ὁ καιρὸς}
\end{array}
$$

When one subordinate element modifies two parallel elements, a line and arrow can be used to show the relationship, as in Mark 1:16a:

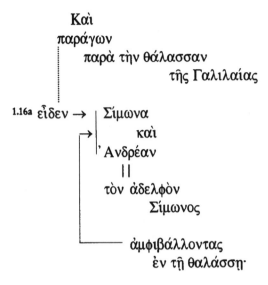

- In elliptical constructions you may choose to supply the implied verb or use a series of dashes (-----) as a way of clarifying the situation, as in Colossians 3:2b below.

3.2b μὴ (φρονειτε) → τὰ
                          ἐπὶ τῆς γῆς.

or

3.2b μὴ ---------- → τὰ
                          ἐπὶ τῆς γῆς.

- You may find a color-coding scheme helpful for clarifying grammatical relationships. Simply choose a color for the various grammatical elements and be consistent. Others prefer to color code rhetorical or thematic features rather than grammatical relationships.

COLOSSIANS 3:1–4 AS EXAMPLE

Grammatical Diagram of Colossians 3:1–4

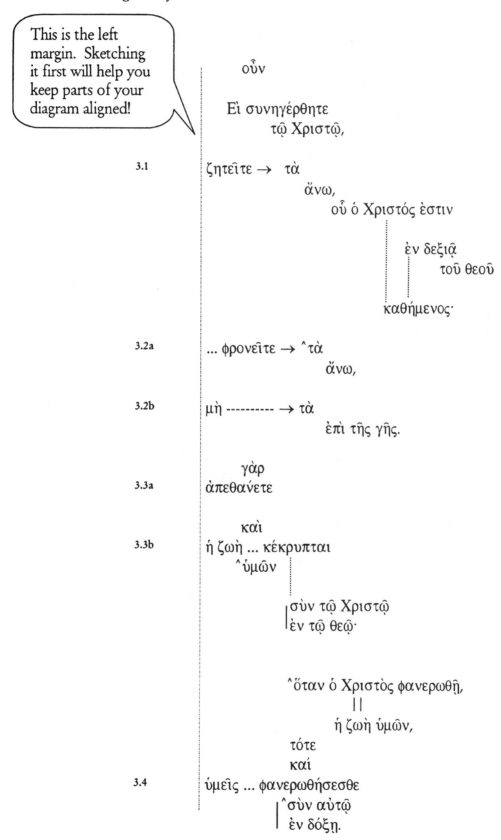

Notes on the Diagram of Colossians 3:1–4

3:1 For the most part the order of the Greek sentence is maintained. There are some exceptions, such as the postpositive coordinate conjunction οὖν in 3:1, which we place five spaces from the far left margin (cf. the other coordinate conjunction in this passage: γὰρ in 3:3a). As you look down the page, the six main clause statements begin at the far left margin (3:1, 2a, 2b, 3a, 3b, 4).

Reading down the page we come to the conditional clause Εἰ συνηγέρθητε. This subordinate expression modifies the main clause verb ζητεῖτε, and for that reason we indent it three spaces from the first letter of that word.

The instrumental dative phrase τῷ Χριστῷ is translated "with Christ" and, since it modifies the verb συνηγέρθητε, is indented three spaces to the right of the first letter in that word. We skip a line after τῷ Χριστῷ and before the main clause. We skip lines after most marks of punctuation and at other times when it helps to prevent confusion.

On the main clause line you will notice that we have pulled the object τὰ ἄνω out of its position and placed it after the verb. We think it is helpful in most cases (cf. also 3:2) to move objects and indirect objects to the right of the verb and to signal this move with an arrow (object/indirect object). If you don't like disturbing word order for this reason, just don't do it. As we said before, feel free to make slight adjustments to the method of diagramming.

The relative clause introduced by οὗ modifies the term ἄνω and is indented three spaces from the first letter of that word. Due to the intervening expression ἐν δεξιᾷ τοῦ θεοῦ, the adjectival participle καθήμενος should not be taken with ἐστιν to form a periphrastic (cf. NIV: "where Christ is seated"), but with Χριστός (NRSV: "where Christ is, seated"). The dotted line clarifies the three-space indention.

We skip a line prior to ἐν δεξιᾷ to prevent confusion. The prepositional phrase ἐν δεξιᾷ appears above the word it modifies, καθήμενος. When modifiers occur before the element they modify, they are diagrammed on the line above. This preserves word order. When they follow the element they modify, they are diagrammed on the line below. Since the genitive expression τοῦ θεοῦ follows and modifies the term δεξιᾷ, we place it on the line below. For both ἐν δεξιᾷ and τοῦ θεοῦ, the three-space indention indicates the subordinate relationship.

3:2 The symbol combination . . . ^ shows that we have moved the object τὰ ἄνω from its original location and placed it to the right of the main verb φρονεῖτε. The arrow also indicates that what follows is an object.

The main clause in 3:2b assumes the main verb φρονεῖτε used above in 3:2a. Sometimes you will be able to identify the understood verb, but not always. When you are unsure of what verb to supply or if you prefer not to supply a verb, you can portray the elliptical situation using a series of dashes (-----).

3:3 We indent the postpositive conjunction γὰρ five spaces from the left margin (the same as οὖν in 3:1). This five-space indention rule for coordinating conjunctions allows you to look down the page and see them in the same column. These conjunctions that join main clause statements will figure prominently in the analysis of semantic structure that follows.

The verb ἀπεθάνετε in 3:3a stands alone but is joined to 3:3b by the coordinating conjunction καὶ. The subject of the main clause in 3:3b, ἡ ζωὴ, is modified by the genitive ὑμῶν, which has been moved from its original location after ζωὴ (notice the . . . ^ indicators) and indented three spaces. Here is another case where you may wish to personalize the method. You may want to leave ὑμῶν where it is since what is gained by the move could be lost by the resulting confusion. The important thing when making personal adjustments is to try to be consistent.

Both prepositional phrases (σὺν τῷ Χριστῷ and ἐν τῷ θεῷ) are shown to modify the main verb κέκρυπται by the three-space indention. The vertical line to the left of the prepositions σὺν and ἐν indicates that the two prepositional phrases are parallel. Some may conclude that the second phrase modifies Χριστῷ rather than κέκρυπται. Notice that a line is skipped before both phrases to prevent the first phrase from appearing on the same line as ὑμῶν.

3:4 A word needs to be said here about the order in which you should read the diagram. As a general rule you should read the diagram from top to bottom until you reach the main clause and then read from left to right. You may encounter a series of elipsis points (. . . .) or the caret (^) as you read down toward the main clause. This tells you that a word, phrase, or clause has been moved out of its original location in the Greek text. Notice, for example, in the diagram of 3:4 that elipsis points follow ὑμεῖς and a caret is in front of σὺν αὐτῷ because the prepositional phrase has been taken out of its place in the main clause and placed on the line below the verb (it is placed on the line below because it follows ὑμεῖς, which begins the main clause).

In diagramming 3:4 we have placed the ὅταν clause in relation to the main verb, φανερωθήσεσθε, by indenting it three spaces on that verb. The phrase ἡ ζωὴ ὑμῶν stands in apposition to Χριστός and explains Christ in relation to Christians; that is, he is "our life." We have found it helpful in appositional situations to place one member directly above the other and mark the relationship using the two vertical lines (||). The word τότε is temporal and also relates to the main verb. Notice that καί here is being understood adjunctively (i.e., "also") and, therefore, is diagrammed as adverbial rather than being placed as a conjunction. The two prepositional phrases σὺν αὐτῷ and ἐν δόξῃ also modify the main verb.

How to Do
Semantic Diagramming

Since the time you were about eighteen months old, you have been working with words, attempting to communicate with others. You began with simple, one-word "requests" or "statements," such as "milk," "more," "outside," "down," and—the bane of parents everywhere—"no!"; but this uncomplicated mode of talking has evolved over the years into more and more complex and effective communication (the complexity seems to peak in the teenage years and again during Ph.D. work!). Presumably, you have learned that good communication involves arranging words, phrases, clauses, sentences, paragraphs, and chapters in ways that make sense and accomplish a desired effect. You have also learned how to understand the written or oral communication of others as you discern how each writer or speaker delivers a given message, crafting language to communicate.

The New Testament text was written to communicate the most important messages of all time. At the beginning of the last section we suggested that grammatical diagramming can serve as a primary tool for clarifying the relationships between words and groups of words in the New Testament. As you learned in that section, grammatical diagramming shows how words, phrases, and clauses relate grammatically within sentences. However, grammatical diagramming cannot depict fully "meaning" relationships or exact functions, and this is where semantic diagramming comes in (the term "semantic" connotes the idea of "meaning"). For example, grammatical diagramming can depict that one part of a sentence is the object of the main clause, but it cannot show how the whole sentence functions in relation to the next sentence. It may be able to show the grammatical relationship between a subordinate, adverbial clause and the main verb, but it cannot depict that the main clause is a command and the adverbial clause gives the "reason" why the reader should obey that command.

The importance of this step in the exegetical process cannot be overemphasized! If you cannot identify the *function* of a word, phrase, clause, or sentence in a passage, your understanding of the passage is limited. On the other hand, learning to diagram the meaning/function relationships between various parts of a passage opens a whole new dimension for clarifying and communicating the text. In fact, our students have said this step, more than any other, has revolutionized both their study and teaching of the New Testament. Although the diagramming described in this section can be intimidating at first glance, we strongly encourage you to take the time to learn the process and struggle with executing your own analysis of passages in the New Testament. You can be sure that the attempt will reward you with greater insight into the text and more effective, exegetically oriented teaching. Our purpose here ultimately is to be better students and teachers of God's Word.

BASIC PRINCIPLES OF SEMANTIC DIAGRAMMING

Our basic approach to semantic diagramming is to depict the meaning/function relationships between the words, phrases, clauses, sentences, and even paragraphs by using lines to the left of our grammatical diagram. The lines show both subordination and the grouping of parts of a passage; they are then "tagged" to show semantic functions.

> *1. Coordinate elements (those that function as "equals" in the passage) are diagrammed with a "half box," as shown below.*

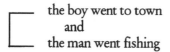

> *2. Subordination is depicted by branching off of the line proceeding from the clause to which another word, phrase, or clause is subordinate.*

You remember from high-school English that clauses are either "independent"—that is, they can stand alone and make sense—or "dependent," playing a supporting role in relation to an independent clause. This dependent relationship is shown as follows.

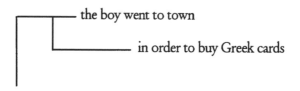

> *3. A semantic function "tag" is placed on the vertical line leading to the sentence element it describes.*

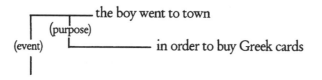

Note: At times a part of the sentence may serve more than one function in the passage. For example, see #45 in the list below, which suggests that elements in Ephesians 5:22–6:9 serve both as exhortations and as an expansion of the discussion. In such a case the tags would be written as "(exhortation/expansion)," showing both functions.

> *4. To mark semantic relationships that involve more than two members, such as sequence, series, or lists, the tag may be written vertically along the vertical line connecting those elements or written to the left of the vertical line.*

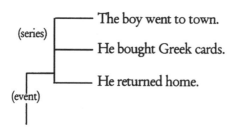

5. *When diagramming elements subordinate to an object, the line branches off the "arrow," pointing at the object.*

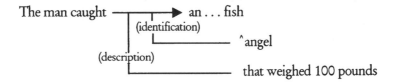

6. *Parallel elements are the one semantic dynamic diagrammed to the right of the text. Parallelism often functions as a style element in a passage and works in conjunction with the logical development of a discussion or narrative. We have found it helpful to diagram parallelism in a manner that allows both style and meaning/function to be depicted at the same time.*

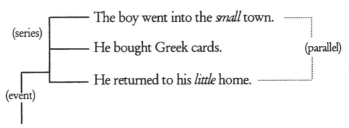

THOUGHTS ON SEMANTIC DIAGRAMMING

1. *As a person who speaks English, you already know intuitively many of the semantic function categories and are learning (or have learned) others in the context of intermediate Greek grammar.*

We have tried to define the functions clearly, steering clear of technical jargon. We also provide examples and give a fairly comprehensive list. The majority of the terms are syntax designations already familiar to anyone who has studied intermediate Greek grammar. An overlap exists between semantic analysis and grammatical analysis. In fact, semantic diagramming incorporates interpretive insights gleaned from Greek syntax studies. All of the remaining designations, such as "introduction," "wish," "idea," "basis," "inference," "restatement," "list," and "sequence," are intuitively understood by most speakers of English. This list is not presented as definitive, but rather as a working model. Feel free to adjust it at points that seem to work better for you. Who knows, you might even discern a "semantic function" in the New Testament that will prove helpful to other students and teachers of Greek!

2. *As you attempt semantic diagramming, you will find yourself struggling with relationships between certain "function" categories listed below; but not only is struggle OK, it is vital to exegesis.*

For example, the delineation of meaning among "motive," "purpose," and "cause" can get a bit messy. The relationship among "explanation," "expansion," and "description" provides another example. Yet in the struggle to identify the best "tag" for a particular part of the Greek text, we are being forced to grapple with the text in meaningful ways. Although the diagramming method itself is fairly simple, discernment of meaning/function relationships in the text offers a stimulating challenge. **We have found it to be the single most dynamic tool to move a student from the nuts and bolts of grammar toward a comprehension of a**

whole passage's structure and message. Such comprehension stands prerequisite to an accurate teaching or preaching of the text.

3. *Begin by diagramming the relationships between subordinate words, phrases, or clauses and those they support. Then deal with the relationships between clauses, sentences, or paragraphs of equal prominence.*

It is important that you begin with a complete grammatical diagram before launching into your semantic diagram. The identification of basic grammatical relationships serves as a foundation to discernment of broader semantic relationships in any passage. Also, the subordinate, or dependent, elements in a passage serve to clarify the clauses they support. If you begin with these subordinate elements, you will have more information for making decisions about the relationships between larger blocks of material.

You are about to embark on an exciting and rewarding aspect of the exegetical process. As we have said before, this method of dealing with the text will pay great dividends if you will give it serious attention. In the first half of *Biblical Greek Exegesis* we begin by including graded assignments on grammatical diagramming. A few months into the process we introduce graded assignments on semantic diagramming. By completing the exercises week by week you will grow in your diagramming skill and realize a new dimension in your study of Scripture.

THE LIST OF SEMANTIC FUNCTIONS

Foundational Expressions

Assertion
Event/Action
Rhetorical Question
Desire (wish/hope)
Exclamation
Exhortation (command/encourage)
Warning
Promise
Problem/Resolution
Entreaty

Related to Events/Actions

Temporal:

Time
Simultaneous
Sequence
Progression

Local:

Place
Sphere
Source
Separation

Other:

Measure
Circumstance
Object (Direct or Indirect)
Cause
Result
Purpose
Means
Manner
Agency
Reference
Advantage or Disadvantage
Association
Relationship
Possession

Argument/Discussion

Logic:

   Basis
   Inference
   Condition
   Concession/Contra-expectation
   Contrast or Comparison
   General/Specific

Clarification:

   Restatement
   Description
   Identification
   Illustration/Example
   Apposition
   Explanation
   Expansion
   Alternative
   Question/Answer
   Content
   Verification

Form:

   Introduction
   Conclusion or Summary
   List
   Series
   Parallel

THE FUNCTIONS DEFINED AND ILLUSTRATED

Foundational Expressions

Foundational expressions (normally main clauses) stand at the heart of any text. The designations below may be used to tag those focal elements in a passage.

1. Assertion

   Ἐγώ εἰμι ἡ ἄμπελος ἡ ἀληθινή.

   I am the true vine. (John 15:1a)

2. Event or Action

   καὶ ἡ ζωὴ ἐφανερώθη.

   And the life was manifested. (1 John 1:2)

3. Rhetorical Question (question used to make a declaration)

   Τίνι γὰρ εἶπέν ποτε τῶν ἀγγέλων, Υἱός μου εἶ σύ;

   For to which of the angels did he ever say, "You are my son"? (Heb. 1:5a)

4. Desire (wish or hope)

   ἐλπίζω δὲ εὐθέως σε ἰδεῖν.

   But I hope to see you soon. (3 John 14a)

5. Exclamation

   ταλαίπωρος ἐγὼ ἄνθρωπος.

   I am a miserable man! (Rom. 7:24a)

6. Exhortation (command or encouragement)

   Ὕπαγε ὀπίσω μου, Σατανᾶ.

   Get behind me Satan! (Mark 8:33)

7. Warning

   Ἑκουσίως γὰρ ἁμαρτανόντων ἡμῶν μετὰ τὸ λαβεῖν τὴν ἐπίγνωσιν τῆς ἀληθείας, οὐκέτι περὶ ἁμαρτιῶν ἀπολείπεται θυσία.

   For if we go on sinning deliberately after receiving a knowledge of the truth, a sacrifice for sins no longer remains. (Heb. 10:26)

8. Promise

   Οὐ μή σε ἀνῶ οὐδ᾽ οὐ μή σε ἐγκαταλίπω.

   I will never leave you, nor will I ever abandon you. (Heb. 13:5b)

9. Problem/Resolution

   Καὶ ὑμᾶς ὄντας νεκροὺς τοῖς παραπτώμασιν καὶ ταῖς ἁμαρτίαις ὑμῶν. . . . ὁ δὲ θεὸς . . . συνεζωοποίησεν τῷ Χριστῷ.

   And you were dead in your wrong deeds and sins. . . . But God . . . made us alive together with Christ. (Eph. 2:1–5)

   The first portion is the "problem" and the second the "resolution."

10. Entreaty

    Τὸν ἄρτον ἡμῶν τὸν ἐπιούσιον δὸς ἡμῖν σήμερον·

    Give us today our daily bread. (Matt.6:11)

Related to Events/Actions[4]

Temporal

11. Time—a simple statement of the time an event, action, or state occurred. It answers the question "When did this occur?"

    <u>τότε νηστεύσαντες καὶ προσευξάμενοι καὶ ἐπιθέντες τὰς χεῖρας</u> αὐτοῖς ἀπέλυσαν.

    <u>Then, when they had fasted and prayed and laid hands on them,</u> they sent them off. (Acts 13:3)

12. Simultaneous—two or more events or states expressed as happening at the same time.

    τότε <u>νηστεύσαντες καὶ προσευξάμενοι</u> καὶ ἐπιθέντες τὰς χεῖρας αὐτοις ἀπέλυσαν.

    Then, when they had <u>fasted and prayed</u> and laid hands on them, they sent them off. (Acts 13:3)

    As shown under "time" in number 11, τότε νηστεύσαντες καὶ προσευξάμενοι communicates time. More specifically, however, the acts of praying and fasting are simultaneous actions within the broader designation of the time of the laying on of hands and sending the apostles off.

13. Sequence—two or more events expressed as happening one after the other.

    Καὶ ὅτι ὤφθη Κηφᾷ <u>εἶτα τοῖς δώδεκα.</u>

    And that he appeared to Cephas, <u>then to the twelve.</u> (1 Cor. 15:5)

14. Progression—same as 13 but the emphasis is placed on the developmental nature of the actions.

    ἐγὼ ἐφύτευσα, <u>Ἀπολλῶς ἐπότισεν.</u>

    I planted, <u>Apollos watered.</u> (1 Cor. 3:6a)

Local

15. Place—where the event, action, or state occurred. Answers the question "Where?"

    ἦλθον <u>εἰς Θεσσαλονίκην.</u>

    They came <u>to Thessalonica.</u>(Acts 17:1b)

16. Sphere—the domain or realm of existence.

    ὑμεῖς δὲ οὐκ ἐστὲ <u>ἐν σαρκὶ</u> ἀλλὰ <u>ἐν πνεύματι.</u>

    But you are not <u>in the flesh,</u> but <u>in the Spirit.</u> (Rom. 8:9a)

    Note: both parts underlined above relate the concept of sphere, but they relate to one another in terms of "contrast" (see #37 below).

---

4. From this point on we underline the part of the text illustrating the category under consideration.

17. Source—the point of origin. Answers the question "From where?"

Ἔχομεν δὲ τὸν θησαυρὸν τοῦτον ἐν ὀστρακίνοις σκεύεσιν, ἵνα ἡ ὑπερβολὴ τῆς δυνάμεως ᾖ <u>τοῦ θεοῦ</u> καὶ μὴ <u>ἐξ ἡμῶν</u>.

Now we have this treasure in "pottery containers," in order that the outstanding quality of the ability (or power) might be <u>from God</u> and not <u>from us</u>. (2 Cor. 4:7)

18. Separation—creating distance between two parties.

καὶ μὴ εἰσενέγκῃς ἡμᾶς εἰς πειρασμόν, ἀλλὰ ῥῦσαι ἡμᾶς <u>ἀπὸ τοῦ πονηροῦ</u>.

And do not lead us into temptation, but deliver us <u>from evil</u>. (Matt. 6:13)

Other

19. Measure—answers the question "How long?" "How many?" or "How far?"

Τί ὧδε ἑστήκατε <u>ὅλην τὴν ἡμέραν</u> ἀργοί;

Why have you been standing here unemployed <u>the whole day</u>? (Matt. 20:6)

20. Circumstance—situations surrounding events or actions.

<u>ἀφέντες πάντα</u> ἠκολούθησαν αὐτῷ.

. . . <u>leaving all</u> they followed him. (Luke 5:11)

21. Object—the receiver of some action (either personal or impersonal). Note: objects are normally diagrammed with the arrow at the end of the main clause. In this case there is no need to add the tag "object" since the element is clearly marked already by an arrow. Objective genitives, on the other hand, are diagrammed on the line below the term they delimit and should be tagged with the term "object."

ὃν προέθετο ὁ θεὸς ἱλαστήριον διὰ τῆς πίστεως ἐν τῷ αὐτοῦ αἵματι εἰς ἔνδειξιν <u>τῆς δικαιοσύνης</u> αὐτοῦ

. . . whom God presented as a propitiation through faith in his blood for a demonstration <u>of his righteousness</u>. (Rom. 3:25)

22. Cause—an event or state that produces some result. Answers the question "What brought this about?"

<u>Δικαιωθέντες</u> οὖν ἐκ πίστεως εἰρήνην ἔχομεν πρὸς τὸν θεὸν διὰ τοῦ κυρίου ἡμῶν Ἰησοῦ Χριστοῦ.

Therefore, <u>having been justified by faith</u>, we have peace with God through our Lord Jesus Christ. (Rom. 5:1a)

23. Result—an outcome of some action or attitude.

καὶ κλείσας τὴν θύραν σου πρόσευξαι τῷ πατρί σου τῷ ἐν τῷ κρυπτῷ· καὶ <u>ὁ πατήρ σου ὁ βλέπων ἐν τῷ κρυπτῷ ἀποδώσει σοι</u>.

And having shut your door, pray to your Father who is in secret, and <u>your Father who sees in secret will repay you</u>. (Matt. 6:6)

24. Purpose—an outcome that one intends to take place or the motive for an action. Answers "What did this person wish to accomplish?" or "Why did he or she do that?"

Οὕτως γὰρ ἠγάπησεν ὁ θεὸς τὸν κόσμον, ὥστε τὸν υἱὸν τὸν μονογενῆ ἔδωκεν, <u>ἵνα πᾶς ὁ πιστεύων εἰς αὐτὸν μὴ ἀπόληται ἀλλ᾽ ἔχῃ ζωὴν αἰώνιον</u>.

For in this way God loved the world, so that he gave his only Son, <u>in order that everyone believing in him may not perish but have eternal life</u>. (John 3:16)

25. Means—the tool or instrument used in carrying out an action. Answers the question "How did this person do that?"

<u>χάριτι δὲ θεοῦ</u> εἰμι ὅ εἰμι.

<u>By the grace of God</u>, I am what I am. (1 Cor. 15:10a)

26. Manner—how the instrument is used. Answers the question "In what way did he do this?"

πλὴν ὅτι <u>παντὶ τρόπῳ</u>, εἴτε προφάσει εἴτε ἀληθείᾳ, Χριστὸς καταγγέλλεται.

Only that <u>in every way</u>, whether with false motives or truth, Christ is being preached (Phil. 1:18)

27. Agency—the personal agent who performs the action. Answers the question "By whom?" or "Through whom?"

εἰρήνην ἔχομεν πρὸς τὸν θεὸν <u>διὰ τοῦ κυρίου ἡμῶν Ἰησοῦ Χριστοῦ</u>.

We have peace with God <u>through our Lord, Jesus Christ</u>. (Rom. 5:1)

28. Reference—an expression of relation. Answers the question "With reference to whom or what?"

ἀποθέσθαι ὑμᾶς <u>κατὰ τὴν προτέραν ἀναστροφὴν</u> τὸν παλαιὸν ἄνθρωπον.

you lay aside <u>with reference to your former way of living</u> the old man. (Eph. 4:22)

29. Advantage/Disadvantage—for whom or against whom an action takes place.

<u>ὑπὲρ</u> γὰρ <u>τοῦ ἀγαθοῦ</u> τάχα τις καὶ τολμᾷ ἀποθανεῖν.

For <u>on behalf of a good person</u> someone might even be brave enough to die. (Rom. 5:7)

30. Association—expresses the idea of accompaniment.

καὶ ὅστις σε ἀγγαρεύσει μίλιον ἕν, ὕπαγε <u>μετ᾽ αὐτοῦ</u> δύο.

And whoever presses you into service for one mile, go <u>with him</u> two. (Matt. 5:41)

31. Relationship—expresses some form of personal relationship.

Εὐχαριστοῦμεν τῷ θεῷ πατρὶ <u>τοῦ κυρίου ἡμῶν</u> Ἰησοῦ Χριστοῦ.

We give thanks to God, the Father <u>of our Lord</u>, Jesus Christ. (Col. 1:3)

32. Possession—expresses ownership.

καὶ τῷ θέλοντί σοι κριθῆναι καὶ τὸν χιτῶνά <u>σου</u> λαβεῖν, ἄφες αὐτῷ καὶ τὸ ἱμάτιον.

And also to the one wishing to sue you and to take <u>your</u> tunic, to him give (<u>your</u>) cloak too. (Matt. 5:40)

Related to Argument/Discussion
Logic

33. Basis—the grounds on which a statement or command is made.

<u>ὁ</u> γὰρ <u>εἰσελθὼν εἰς τὴν κατάπαυσιν αὐτοῦ καὶ αὐτὸς κατέπαυσεν ἀπὸ τῶν ἔργων αὐτοῦ</u>

ὥσπερ ἀπὸ τῶν ἰδίων ὁ θεός. σπουδάσωμεν οὖν εἰσελθεῖν εἰς ἐκείνην τὴν κατάπαυσιν.

For <u>the one having entered into his rest also has rested from his own works as God did from his</u>. Therefore, let us strive to enter that rest. (Heb. 4:10–11)

34. Inference—the logical conclusion drawn from an assertion.

    εἴ τις ἐν λόγῳ οὐ πταίει, <u>οὗτος τέλειος ἀνήρ</u>.

    If anyone does not stumble in speech, <u>this one is a mature person.</u> (James 3:2)

35. Condition—a requirement

    <u>εἴ τις ἐν λόγῳ οὐ πταίει,</u> οὗτος τέλειος ἀνήρ.

    <u>If anyone does not stumble in speech,</u> this one is a mature person. (James 3:2)

36. Concession/Contra-expectation—a reservation or qualification ("although")/an unexpected outcome or truth ("sweet surprise").

    <u>καίπερ ὢν υἱός,</u> <u>ἔμαθεν ἀφ' ὧν ἔπαθεν τὴν ὑπακοήν</u>.

    <u>Although he was a Son,</u> <u>he learned obedience from the things he suffered</u>. (Heb. 5:8)

    The first part of the verse is the concession; the second is the contra-expectation.

37. Contrast/Comparison—two conditions, ideas, or actions put together in order to point out differences or similarities.

    διὰ τοῦτο <u>μὴ γίνεσθε ἄφρονες</u>, ἀλλὰ <u>συνίετε τί τὸ θέλημα τοῦ κυρίου</u>.

    For this reason <u>do not be foolish</u>, but <u>discern what the will of the Lord is</u>. (Eph. 5:17)

    This verse illustrates contrast.

38. General/Specific—the juxtaposition of "general" and "specific" shows the relationship between a broader and a more particular concept, truth, or action.

    <u>καὶ οὐχ ἑαυτῷ τις λαμβάνει τὴν τιμὴν</u> ἀλλὰ καλούμενος ὑπὸ τοῦ θεοῦ καθώσπερ καὶ Ἀαρών. Οὕτως καὶ <u>ὁ Χριστὸς οὐχ ἑαυτὸν ἐδόξασεν γενηθῆναι ἀρχιερέα</u>.

    <u>And no one grabs this honor for himself,</u> but being called by God even as Aaron was. So also <u>Christ did not glorify himself to become a high priest</u>. (Heb. 5:4–5)

    The first underlined portion asserts a general truth; the second shows that this truth relates specifically to Christ.

Clarification

39. Restatement—the same idea is expressed in a different way.

    ἵλεως ἔσομαι ταῖς ἀδικίαις αὐτῶν καὶ <u>τῶν ἁμαρτιῶν αὐτῶν οὐ μὴ μνησθῶ ἔτι</u>.

    I will be merciful towards their unrighteous acts, and <u>I will no longer remember their sins</u>. (Heb. 8:12)

    The second promise is a restatement of the first. Notice that when the author alludes to this Old Testament verse (Jer. 31:34) again, the two parts are melded (see Heb. 10:17)

40. Description—functions to provide vivid detail of a person, event, state, or object.

    καὶ ἰδοὺ δράκων <u>μέγας πυρρὸς</u> <u>ἔχων κεφαλὰς ἑπτὰ καὶ κέρατα δέκα.</u>

    And behold a <u>large red</u> dragon <u>having seven heads and ten horns</u>. (Rev. 12:3)

41. Identification—information used to specify a person or thing. Answers the question "Which one?"

    Ἦν δὲ ἄνθρωπος ἐκ τῶν Φαρισαίων, <u>Νικόδημος ὄνομα αὐτῷ,</u> ἄρχων τῶν Ἰουδαίων.

    Now there was a man who was a member of the Pharisees, <u>Nicodemus by name</u>, who was a ruler of the Jews. (John 3:1)

42. Illustration (or Example)—material used to elucidate by use of an example.

    μιμηταὶ δὲ τῶν διὰ πίστεως καὶ μακροθυμίας κληρονομούντων τὰς ἐπαγγελίας. <u>Τῷ γὰρ Ἀβραὰμ ἐπαγγειλάμενος ὁ θεός … ὤμοσεν καθ᾽ ἑαυτοῦ … καὶ οὕτως μακροθυμήσας ἐπέτυχεν τῆς ἐπαγγελίας.</u>

    But (be) imitators of those who through faith and patience inherit the promises. <u>For God, having promised to Abraham … swore by himself …. And so having waited patiently [Abraham] obtained the promise.</u> (Heb. 6:12–15)

    The whole of vv. 13–15 functions as the illustration.

43. Apposition—a noun or participle that follows immediately another noun or participle with which it shares a common referent. Note: the grammatical diagram marks appositional elements with vertical parallel lines. Thus there is no need to "tag" this dynamic with the word "apposition" since it is clearly marked already.

    Τούτου χάριν ἐγὼ Παῦλος <u>ὁ δέσμιος</u> τοῦ Χριστοῦ [Ἰησοῦ] ὑπὲρ ὑμῶν τῶν ἐθνῶν.

    For this reason I, Paul, <u>the prisoner</u> of Christ Jesus on behalf of you Gentiles. (Eph. 3:1)

    At first glace you may think of "the prisoner" as identification, but the readers already know he is in prison. Rather, the apostle uses these terms appositionally for stylistic effect.

44. Explanation—the addition of clarifying statements to a main proposition or command.

    Προσευχόμενοι δὲ μὴ βατταλογήσητε ὥσπερ οἱ ἐθνικοί, <u>δοκοῦσιν γὰρ ὅτι ἐν τῇ πολυλογίᾳ αὐτῶν εἰσακουσθήσονται.</u>

    But as you are praying, do not babble like the Gentiles, <u>for they think that by their many words they will be heard.</u> (Matt. 6:7)

    The underlined portion of the sentence explains why the Gentiles babble.

45. Expansion—further development of an idea, addition of a related concept, or concepts to a discussion. Sometimes the main points of a discussion will constitute an expansion.

    Αἱ γυναῖκες τοῖς ἰδίοις ἀνδράσιν ὡς τῷ κυρίῳ …

    Οἱ ἄνδρες, ἀγαπᾶτε τὰς γυναῖκας …

    Τὰ τέκνα, ὑπακούετε τοῖς γονεῦσιν ὑμῶν …

    Καὶ οἱ πατέρες, μὴ παροργίζετε τὰ τέκνα ὑμῶν …

    Οἱ δοῦλοι, ὑπακούετε τοῖς κατὰ σάρκα κυρίοις …

    Καὶ οἱ κύριοι, τὰ αὐτὰ ποιεῖτε πρὸς αὐτούς …

    Wives, (submit) to your husbands, as to the Lord …

    Husbands, love your wives …

    Children, obey your parents …

And, fathers, do not exasperate your children . . .

Slaves, obey your human masters . . .

And masters, do the same (i.e., act with good will) to them . . . (Eph. 5:22–6:9)

Each of these are exhortations (see 6), but they also expand the discussion. The whole passage also serves as giving specific (see 38) teaching on the general exhortation in 5:21.

46. Alternative (either . . . or)—when one condition, action, or place is expressed as a possible substitute for another.

ἢ γὰρ τὸν ἕνα μισήσει καὶ τὸν ἕτερον ἀγαπήσει, <u>ἢ ἑνὸς ἀνθέξεται καὶ τοῦ ἑτέρου</u> <u>καταφρονήσει</u>.

For either he will hate the one and love the other, <u>or he will be loyal to the one and treat the other with contempt</u>. (Matt. 6:24)

47. Question/Answer—an expression of inquiry and the response to an inquiry.

καὶ αὐτὸς ἐπηρώτα αὐτούς, <u>Ὑμεῖς δὲ τίνα με λέγετε εἶναι;</u> ἀποκριθεὶς ὁ Πέτρος λέγει αὐτῷ, <u>Σὺ εἶ ὁ Χριστός</u>.

And he asked them, "<u>Who do you say that I am?</u>" Peter answering said to him, "<u>You are the Messiah</u>." (Mark 8:29)

48. Content—an explication of the makeup of a concept or discussion.

Διὸ ἀφέντες τὸν τῆς ἀρχῆς τοῦ Χριστοῦ λόγον · μὴ πάλιν θεμέλιον καταβαλλόμενοι <u>μετανοίας ἀπὸ νεκρῶν ἔργων καὶ πίστεως ἐπὶ θεόν, βαπτισμῶν διδαχῆς ἐπιθέσεώς τε</u> <u>χειρῶν</u>.

Therefore, moving on from the elementary teaching about Christ . . . not putting down a foundation again of <u>repentance from dead works, and of faith in God, of teaching about baptisms, and of laying on of hands</u>. (Heb. 6:1–2)

The underlined section gives the content of the "elementary teaching."

49. Verification—shows the validity of an assertion by providing some form of corroborating evidence.

οὐ γὰρ Δαυὶδ ἀνέβη εἰς τοὺς οὐρανούς, <u>λέγει δὲ αὐτός, Εἶπεν [ὁ] κύριος τῷ κυρίῳ μου,</u> <u>Κάθου ἐκ δεξιῶν μου, ἕως ἂν θῶ τοὺς ἐχθρούς σου ὑποπόδιον τῶν ποδῶν σου</u>.

For it was not David who ascended into the heavens, but he says himself: "<u>The Lord said to my Lord, 'Sit at my right hand until I make your enemies a footstool for your feet.'</u>" (Acts 2:34–35)

Here Peter uses Psalm 110:1 to verify his assertion about Jesus' exaltation.

Form

50. Introduction—a passage that presents the opening of a discussion, letter, or narrative.

<u>Ἀρχὴ τοῦ εὐαγγελίου Ἰησοῦ Χριστοῦ [υἱοῦ θεοῦ]</u>.

<u>The beginning of the gospel of Jesus Christ, the Son of God</u>. (Mark 1:1)

51. Conclusion or Summary—a passage that brings to an end by way of summary or final decisive statement.

<u>Καὶ ἐγένετο ὅτε ἐτέλεσεν ὁ Ἰησοῦς τοὺς λόγους τούτους, ἐξεπλήσσοντο οἱ ὄχλοι ἐπὶ τῇ διδαχῇ αὐτοῦ· ἦν γὰρ διδάσκων αὐτοὺς ὡς ἐξουσίαν ἔχων.</u>

<u>And it came about when Jesus finished these words, the crowds were astounded at his teaching. For he taught them as one having authority.</u> (Matt. 7:28–29)

The whole of this passage serves as the conclusion to the Sermon on the Mount.

52. List—a number of things, normally of the same kind, mentioned one after the other.

τὸ δὲ τέλος τῆς παραγγελίας ἐστὶν <u>ἀγάπη ἐκ καθαρᾶς καρδίας</u> καὶ <u>συνειδήσεως ἀγαθῆς</u> καὶ <u>πίστεως ἀνυποκρίτου.</u>

But the outcome of our instruction is <u>love that flows from a pure heart</u>, and <u>a good conscience</u>, and <u>a sincere faith</u>. (1 Tim. 1:5)

53. Series—the joining of equally prominent assertions or commands in a loose association. Answers the question "What is the next point?" (These are more loosely associated than "expansion")

<u>Πάντοτε χαίρετε, ἀδιαλείπτως προσεύχεσθε, ἐν παντὶ εὐχαριστεῖτε.</u>

<u>Rejoice always. Pray constantly. In all things give thanks.</u> (1 Thess. 5:16–18)

These are three conjoined exhortations that do not expand a single concept but provide a series of ideas.

54. Parallel—two or more elements correspond verbally or conceptually.

<u>Ὑμεῖς ἐστε</u> τὸ ἅλας τῆς γῆς. . . . <u>Ὑμεῖς ἐστε</u> τὸ φῶς τοῦ κόσμου.

<u>You are</u> the salt of the earth. . . . <u>You are</u> the light of the world. (Matt. 5:13–14)

Remember that parallels are diagrammed to the right of the text.

COLOSSIANS 1:3–5A AS EXAMPLE

Colossians 1:3–5a

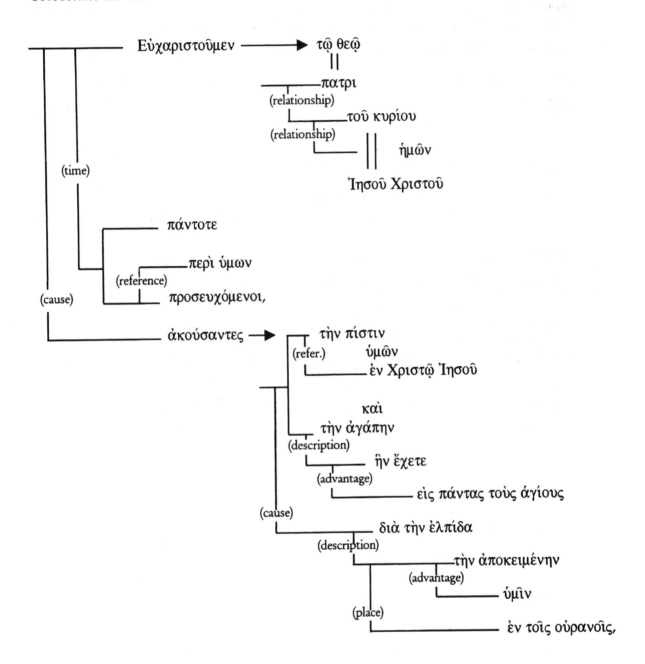

Syntax and Diagramming Exercises

1 JOHN 1:1–2:2; 2:28–3:10

1 John 1:1–4

Syntax

1. ἑωράκαμεν (1)	(tense)	_____
2. ὀφθαλμοῖς (1)	Instrumental dative of means	
3. ζωῆς (1)	(case)	_____
4. ζωὴ (2)	(case)	_____
5. ὑμῖν (2)	(case)	_____
6. second καὶ (3)	(function)	_____
7. κοινωνίαν (3)	(case)	_____

Diagramming[5]—1 John 1:2: καὶ ἀπαγγέλλομεν ὑμῖν τὴν ζωὴν τὴν αἰώνιον

Vocabulary—(Your teacher will make weekly assignments.)

---

5. All diagramming assignments will involve grammatical diagramming until we begin to work with Colossians, at which point semantic diagramming will be added.

1 John 1:5–2:2

Syntax

1. αὐτοῦ (5) (case) _____
2. φῶς (5) (case) _____
3. <u>οὐκ . . . οὐδεμία</u> (5) <u>Double negative</u>
4. <u>εἴπωμεν</u> (6) <u>Subjunctive in a conditional sentence</u>
5. σκότει (6) (case) _____
6. ἀλλήλων (7) (case) _____
7. υἱοῦ (7) (case) _____
8. ἁμαρτίας (7) (case) _____
9. ἀφῇ (9) (mood) _____
10. ἡμαρτήκαμεν (10) (tense) _____
11. τὸν (1) (function) _____
12. Ἰησοῦν Χριστὸν (1) (case) _____

Diagramming—1 John 1:5a: Καὶ ἔστιν αὕτη ἡ ἀγγελία ἣν ἀκηκόαμεν ἀπ᾽ αὐτοῦ καὶ ἀναγγέλλομεν ὑμῖν,

Vocabulary—

1 John 2:28–3:3

Syntax

1. μένετε (28)   (mood) _____
2. σχῶμεν (28)   (mood) _____
3. παρουσίᾳ (28)   (case) _____
4. δίκαιός (29)   (case) _____
5. δικαιοσύνην (29)   (case) _____
6. τέκνα (1)   (case) _____
7. τοῦτο (1)   (case) _____
8. ὅμοιοι (2)   (function) _____
9. second ἐσόμεθα (2)   (tense) _____

Diagramming—1 John 2:28

Vocabulary—

1 John 3:4–10

Syntax

1. ἀνομίαν (4)   (case) _____
2. ὅτι clause (5)   (function) _____
3. αὐτῷ (5)   (case) _____
4. ἁμαρτάνει (6)   (tense) _____
6. ἁμαρτάνων (6)   (function) _____
5. πλανάτω (7)   (mood) _____
7. καθὼς clause (7)   (function) _____
8. διαβόλου (8)   (case) _____
9. ἁμαρτάνει (8)   (tense) _____
10. ποιεῖ (9)   (tense) _____
11. ἁμαρτάνειν (9)   (function) _____
12. τούτῳ (10)   (case) _____

Diagramming—1 John 3:5

Vocabulary—

JOHN 15:1–27

John 15:1–4

Syntax

1. ἀληθινή (1)   (function) _____

2. μου (1)   (case) _____

3. κλῆμα (2)   (case) _____

4. φέρον (2)   (function) _____

5. <u>αἴρει</u> (2)   <u>Iterative present or gnomic present</u>

6. φέρῃ (2)   (mood) _____

7. λόγον (3)   (case) _____

8. <u>λελάληκα</u> (3)   <u>Intensive perfect</u>

9. μείνατε (4)   (tense) _____

10. φέρειν (4)   (function) _____

11. ἑαυτοῦ (4)   (case) _____

12. μένητε (4)   (mood) _____

Diagramming—John 15:1, 3

Vocabulary—

John 15:5–11

Syntax

1. μένων (5)   (function) _____
2. ἐμοῦ (5)   (case) _____
3. οὐ … οὐδέν (5)   (construction) _____
4. ἐμοί (6)   (case) _____
5. ἐβλήθη & ἐξηράνθη (6) (tense) _____
6. <u>συνάγουσιν</u> (6)   <u>Customary present</u>
7. πῦρ (6)   (case) _____
8. <u>ὑμῖν</u> (7)   <u>Dative of advantage</u>
9. τούτῳ (8)   (case) _____
10. φέρητε (8)   (mood) _____
11. ἐμοὶ (8)   (case) _____
12. first μου (10)   (case) _____
13. τετήρηκα (10)   (tense) _____

Diagramming—John 15:10

Vocabulary—

John 15:12–17

Syntax

1. ἀγαπᾶτε (12)   (mood) _____
2. ταύτης (13)   (case) _____
3. φίλων (13)   (case) _____
4. ὑμῖν (14)   (case) _____
5. <u>ὑμᾶς δούλους</u> (15)   <u>Double accusative</u>
6. ὅτι clause (15)   (function) _____
7. ἤκουσα (15)   (mood) _____
8. πατρός (15)   (case) _____
9. ἐξελεξάμην (16)   (tense) _____
10. δῷ (16)   (mood) _____

Diagramming—John 15:14–15a

Vocabulary—

John 15:18–21

Syntax

1.	<u>Εἰ . . ., . . . (18)</u>	<u>First class conditional sentence</u>
2.	ὑμῶν (18)	(case) _____
3.	<u>εἰ . . ., ἄν . . . (19)</u>	<u>Second class conditional sentence</u>
4.	κόσμου (19)	(case) _____
5.	μισεῖ (19)	(tense) _____
6.	λόγου (20)	(case) _____
7.	κυρίου (20)	(case) _____
8.	ὑμᾶς (21)	(case) _____
9.	πέμψαντά (21)	(function) _____

Diagramming—John 15:18, 21

Vocabulary—

John 15:22–27

Syntax

1. ἁμαρτίας (22)   (case) _____
2. αὐτοῖς (24)   (case) _____
3. ἑωράκασιν (24)   (tense) _____
4. second ὁ (25)   (function) _____
5. ὅτι (25)   (function) _____
6. δωρεάν (25)   (case) _____
7. ἀληθείας (26)   (case) _____
8. ἐμοῦ (26)   (case) _____
9. ἀρχῆς (27)   (case) _____
10. ἐμοῦ (27)   (case) _____
11. ἐστε (27)   (tense) _____

Diagramming—John 15:22, 24

Vocabulary—

MARK 1:1–28

Mark 1:1–4

Syntax

1. Ἀρχὴ (1)   (case) _____

2. Ἰησοῦ Χριστοῦ (1)   (case) _____

3. [υἱοῦ θεοῦ] (1)   (case) _____

4. <u>γέγραπται</u> (2)   <u>Consummative perfect</u>

5. προφήτῃ (2)   (case) _____

6. σου (2)   (case) _____

7. φωνὴ (3)   (case) _____

8. ἐρήμῳ (3)   (case) _____

9. <u>βαπτίζων</u> (4)   <u>Participle: attributive (with the article) or</u>

                           <u>adverbial (circumstantial)-manner</u>

10. μετανοίας (4)   (case) _____

11. ἄφεσιν (4)   (case) _____

Diagramming—Mark 1:2b–3

Vocabulary—

Mark 1:5–8

Syntax

1. ἐξεπορεύετο (5)   (tense) _____

2. αὐτοῦ (5)   (case) _____

3. <u>ἐξομολογούμενοι</u> (5)   <u>Participle: attendant circumstance</u>

4. ἦν . . . ἐνδεδυμένος (6)   (construction) _____

5. ὀσφὺν (6)   (case) _____

6. <u>λέγων</u> (7)   <u>Participle: redundant</u>

7. first μου (7)   (case) _____

8. κύψας (7)   (function) _____

9. λῦσαι (7)   (function) _____

10. ἐβάπτισα (8)   (tense) _____

11. βαπτίσει (8)   (tense) _____

12. πνεύματι (8)   (case) _____

Diagramming—Mark 1:5

Vocabulary—

Mark 1:9–13

Syntax

1. ταῖς (9)   (function) _____

2. ἐβαπτίσθη (9)   (tense) _____

3. Ἰωάννου (9)   (case) _____

4. ἀναβαίνων (10)   (function) _____

5. σχιζομένους (10)   (function) _____

6. οὐρανοὺς (10)   (case) _____

7. ἀγαπητός (11)   (case) _____

8. <u>ἡμέρας</u> (13)   <u>Accusative of measure</u>

9. <u>πειραζόμενος</u> (13) <u>Participle: adverbial—purpose</u>

10. Σατανᾶ (13)   (case) _____

11. θηρίων (13)   (case) _____

Diagramming—Mark 1:10

Vocabulary—

Mark 1:14–20

Syntax

1. παραδοθῆναι (14)   (function) _____
2. Ἰωάννην (14)   (case) _____
3. κηρύσσων (14)   (function) _____
4. <u>ὅτι</u> (15)   <u>Content conjunction (ὅτι recitativum)</u>
5. ἤγγικεν (15)   (tense) _____
6. τοῦ (15)   (function) _____
7. ἀδελφὸν (16)   (case) _____
8. ποιήσω (17)   (voice) _____
9. ὑμᾶς (17)   (case) _____
10. ἁλιεῖς (17)   (case) _____
11. ἀφέντες (18)   (function) _____
12. ὀλίγον (19)   (function) _____
13. <u>τοῦ</u> (19)   <u>Genitive of relationship</u>

Diagramming—Mark 1:14–15

Vocabulary—

Mark 1:21–24

Syntax

1. εἰσπορεύονται (21)   (tense) _____
2. <u>σάββασιν</u> (21)   <u>Local dative of time</u>
3. ἐδίδασκεν (21)   (tense) _____
4. διδαχῇ (22)   (case) _____
5. ἦν … διδάσκων (22)   (construction) _____
6. ἔχων (22)   (function) _____
7. πνεύματι (23)   (case) _____
8. λέγων (24)   (function) _____
9. ἡμῖν καὶ σοί (24)   (case) _____
10. Ἰησοῦ (24)   (case) _____
11. ἦλθες (24)   (mood) _____
12. <u>ἀπολέσαι</u> (24)   <u>Infinitive: adverbial-purpose</u>

Diagramming—Mark 1:21–22

Vocabulary—

Mark 1:25–28

Syntax

1. αὐτῷ (25)   (case) _____

2. Φιμώθητι (25)   (mood) _____

3. σπαράξαν (26)   (function) _____

4. ἀκάθαρτον (26)   (function) _____

5. φωνῇ (26)   (case) _____

6. <u>συζητεῖν</u> (27)   <u>Infinitive: adverbial-result</u>

7. ἑαυτοὺς (27)   (case) _____

8. ἐξουσίαν (27)   (case) _____

9. αὐτοῦ (28)   (case) _____

Diagramming—Mark 1:25–26

Vocabulary—

MARK 8:27–9:8

Mark 8:27–32

Syntax

1. με (27)	Accusative: subject of an infinitive
2. οἱ (28)	Article functioning as a personal pronoun
3. λέγοντες (28)	(function) _____
4. προφητῶν (28)	Partitive genitive
5. ἐπηρώτα (29)	(tense) _____
6. εἶναι (29)	(function) _____
7. ἀποκριθεὶς (29)	(function) _____
8. λέγει (29)	(tense) _____
9. ἵνα clause (30)	(function) _____
10. διδάσκειν (31)	Infinitive: adverbial-complementary
11. παθεῖν (31)	(function) _____
12. πρεσβυτέρων (31)	(case) _____
13. παρρησίᾳ (32)	(case) _____
14. προσλαβόμενος (32)	(function) _____

Diagramming—Mark 8:31

Vocabulary—

Mark 8:33–9:1

Syntax

1. λέγει (33)   <u>Historical present</u>
2. φρονεῖς (33)   (tense) _____
3. μαθηταῖς (34)   (case) _____
4. Εἴ ... θέλει (34)   (construction) _____
5. ἀκολουθείτω (34)   (tense) _____
6. θέλῃ (35)   (mood) _____
7. ἀπολέσει (35)   (tense) _____
8. ἐμοῦ (35)   (case) _____
9. καὶ (36)   (function) _____
10. δοῖ (37)   <u>Deliberative subjunctive</u>
11. second τῶν (38)   (function) _____
12. ἑστηκότων (1)   (case) _____
13. οὐ μὴ γεύσωνται (1)   <u>Subjunctive/emphatic negation</u>
14. ἴδωσιν (1)   (mood) _____

Diagramming—Mark 8:34

Vocabulary—

Mark 9:2–8

Syntax

1. παραλαμβάνει (2)   (tense) _____
2. στίλβοντα (3)   (function) _____
3. ἦσαν συλλαλοῦντες (4)   (construction) _____
4. ἡμᾶς (5)   (case) _____
5. εἶναι (5)   (function) _____
6. <u>ποιήσωμεν</u> (5)   <u>Hortatory subjunctive</u>
7. σοὶ (5)   (case) _____
8. ἐπισκιάζουσα (7)   (function) _____
9 ἀγαπητός (7)   (function) _____
10. αὐτοῦ (7)   (case) _____
11. περιβλεψάμενοι (8)   (function) _____
12. ἀλλὰ (8)   (function) _____

Diagramming—Mark 9:7–8

Vocabulary—

COLOSSIANS 1:1–23

Colossians 1:1–8

Syntax

1. θελήματος (1)   (case) _____
2. ἀδελφὸς (1)   (case) _____
3. Χριστῷ (2)   (case) _____
4. χάρις (2)   (case) _____
5. Εὐχαριστοῦμεν (3)   (tense) _____
6. ὑμῶν (3)   (case) _____
7. προσευχόμενοι (3)   (function) _____
8. ἀκούσαντες (4)   (function) _____
9. ἀποκειμένην (5)   (function) _____
10. <u>ἀληθείας</u> (5)   <u>Hebraic genitive or attributive genitive</u>
11. ἐστὶν καρποφορούμενον (6) (construction) _____
12. <u>ἐπέγνωτε</u> (6)   <u>Ingressive aorist</u>
13. ἐμάθετε (7)   (tense) _____

Diagramming—Col. 1:3–4 (grammatical and semantic)

Vocabulary—

Colossians 1:9–14

Syntax

1. τοῦτο (9)   (case)_____

2. ἵνα (9)   (construction) _____

3. <u>ἐπίγνωσιν</u> (9)   <u>Accusative of reference (respect)</u> or content

4. περιπατῆσαι (10)   (function) _____

5. κυρίου (10)   (case)_____

6. καρποφοροῦντες (10)   (function) _____

7. <u>ἐπιγνώσει</u> (10)   <u>Dative of reference</u>

8. θεοῦ (10)   (case)_____

9. δόξης (11)   (case)_____

10. ὑπομονὴν (11)   (case)_____

11. χαρᾶς (11)   (case)_____

12. κλήρου (12)   (case)_____

13. ἀγάπης (13)   (case)_____

Diagramming—Col. 1:9 (grammatical and semantic)

Vocabulary—

Colossians 1:15–20

Syntax

1. εἰκὼν (15)   (case) _____

2. κτίσεως (15)   (case) _____

3. αὐτῷ (16)   (case) _____

4. αὐτοῦ (16)   (case) _____

5. ἔκτισται (16)   (tense) _____

6. πάντων (17)   (case) _____

7. πάντα (17)   (case) _____

8. ἐκκλησίας (18)   (case) _____

9. πρωτεύων (18)   (function) _____

10. εὐδόκησεν (19)   (tense) _____

11. εἰρηνοποιήσας (20)   (function) _____

12. γῆς (20)   (case) _____

Diagramming—Col. 1:18–19 (grammatical and semantic)

Vocabulary—

Colossians 1:21–23

Syntax

1. ὄντας ἀπηλλοτριωμένους (21) (construction) _____
2. διανοίᾳ (21)   (case) _____
3. ἔργοις (21)   (case) _____
4. ἀποκατήλλαξεν (22)   (tense) _____
5. σαρκὸς (22)   (case) _____
6. θανάτου (22)   (case) _____
7. παραστῆσαι (22)   (function) _____
8. ἐπιμένετε (23)   (tense) _____
9. τεθεμελιωμένοι (23)   (function) _____
10. ἐλπίδος (23)   (case) _____
11. ἠκούσατε (23)   (tense) _____
12. second τοῦ (23)   (function) _____
13. διάκονος (23)   (case) _____

Diagramming—Col. 1:22 (grammatical and semantic)

Vocabulary—

MATTHEW 6:5–34

Matthew 6:5–8

Syntax

1. προσεύχησθε (5)   (mood) _____
2. <u>ἔσεσθε</u> (5)   <u>Imperatival future</u> (mood) _____
3. πλατειῶν (5)   (case) _____
4. ἑστῶτες (5)   (function) _____
5. <u>προσεύχεσθαι</u> (5)   <u>Infinitive: adverbial-complementary</u>
6. φανῶσιν (5)   (mood) _____
7. <u>ἀνθρώποις</u> (5)   <u>Instrumental dative of agency</u>
8. προσεύχῃ (6)   (mood) _____
9. κλείσας (6)   (function) _____
10. βλέπων (6)   (function) _____
11. Προσευχόμενοι (7)   (function) _____
12. <u>βατταλογήσητε</u> (7)   <u>Prohibitive subjunctive</u>
13. πολυλογίᾳ (7)   (case) _____
14. ὁμοιωθῆτε (8)   (mood) _____
15. ὑμᾶς (8)   (case) _____

Diagramming—Matt. 6:6–7 (grammatical and semantic)

Vocabulary—

Matthew 6:9–15

Syntax

1. προσεύχεσθε (9)   (tense) _____
2. ἡμῶν (9)   (case) _____
3. ὁ (9)   (function) _____
4. <u>ἁγιασθήτω</u> (9)   <u>Imperative of entreaty (request)</u>
5. second τὸν (11)   (function) _____
6. ἡμῖν (12)   (case) _____
7. ἀφήκαμεν (12)   (tense) _____
8. ὀφειλέταις (12)   (case) _____
9. εἰσενέγκῃς (13)   (mood) _____
10. <u>πονηροῦ</u> (13) <u>Substantival adjective</u>
11. Ἐὰν ... ἀφῆτε (14)   (construction) _____
12. ἀφήσει (14)   (tense) _____
13. ἀνθρώποις (15)   (case) _____

Diagramming—Matt. 6:9–13 (grammatical and semantic)

Vocabulary—

Matthew 6:16–21

Syntax

1. νηστεύητε (16)   (function) _____
2. σκυθρωποί (16)   (function) _____
3. φανῶσιν (16)   (mood) _____
4. νηστεύοντες (16)   (function) _____
5. νηστεύων (17)   (function) _____
6. ἀνθρώποις (18)   (case) _____
7. second τῷ (18)   (function) _____
8. ὑμῖν (19)   (case) _____
9. θησαυροὺς (19)   (case) _____
10. ἀφανίζει (19)   (tense) _____
11. θησαυρίζετε (20)   (tense) _____
12. καρδία (21)   (case) _____

Diagramming—Matt. 6:19–21 (grammatical and semantic)

Vocabulary—

Matthew 6:22–26

Syntax

1. ὀφθαλμός (22)   (case) _____
2. ἐὰν . . . ᾖ (23)   (construction) _____
3. δουλεύειν (24)   (function) _____
4. ἕνα (24)   (function) _____
5. <u>μισήσει</u> (24)   <u>Gnomic future</u>
6. τοῦτο (25)   (case) _____
7. μὴ μεριμνᾶτε (25)   (construction) _____
8. ψυχῇ (25)   (case) _____
9. φάγητε (25)   (mood) _____
10. τροφῆς (25)   (case) _____
11. πετεινὰ (26)   (case) _____
12. ὅτι (26)   (function) _____
13. καὶ (26)   (function) _____

Diagramming—Matt. 6:22–24 (grammatical and semantic)

Vocabulary—

Matthew 6:27–34

Syntax

1. ὑμῶν (27)   (case) _____

2. μεριμνῶν (27)   <u>Participle: adverbial-instrumental</u>

3. ἐνδύματος (28) (case) _____

4. <u>περιεβάλετο</u> (29) <u>Direct (or reflexive) middle</u>

5. θεὸς (30)   (case) _____

6. πολλῷ (30)   (case) _____

7. φάγωμεν (31)   (mood) _____

8. ἐπιζητοῦσιν (32) (tense) _____

9. ζητεῖτε (33)   (mood) _____

10. προστεθήσεται (33) (tense) _____

11. μεριμνήσητε (34) (mood) _____

12. εἰς (34)   (function) _____

13. <u>αὐτῆς</u> (34)   <u>Genitive of possession</u>

Diagramming—Matt. 6:31–33 (grammatical and semantic)

Vocabulary—

ROMANS 3:21–26; 5:1–11; 8:1–17

Romans 3:21–26

Syntax

1. νόμου (21)   (case) _____
2. θεοῦ (21)   (case) _____
3. πεφανέρωται (21)   (mood) _____
4. μαρτυρουμένη (21)   (function) _____
5. πίστεως (22)   (case) _____
6. Ἰησοῦ Χριστοῦ (22)   (case) _____
7. ἥμαρτον (23)   (tense) _____
8. δόξης (23)   (case) _____
9. δικαιούμενοι (24)   (function) _____
10. χάριτι (24)   (case) _____
11. second τῆς (24)   (function) _____
12. προγεγονότων (25)   (function) _____
13. τὴν (26)   Anaphoric use of the article
14. εἰς τὸ εἶναι (26)   (function) _____

Diagramming—Rom. 3:23–26 (grammatical and semantic)

Vocabulary—

Romans 5:1–5

Syntax

    1. Δικαιωθέντες (1)   (function) _____

    2. Ἰησοῦ Χριστοῦ (1)   (case) _____

    3. ἐσχήκαμεν (2)   (tense) _____

    4. χάριν (2)   (case) _____

    5. καυχώμεθα (2)   (mood) _____

    6. εἰδότες (3)   (function) _____

    7. κατεργάζεται (3)   (tense) _____

    8. δοκιμήν (4)   (case) _____

    9. θεοῦ (5)   (case) _____

    10. ἐκκέχυται (5)   (tense) _____

    11. πνεύματος (5)   (case) _____

    12. δοθέντος (5)   (function) _____

Diagramming—Rom. 5:1–4 (grammatical and semantic)

Vocabulary—

Romans 5:6–11

Syntax

1. ὄντων ἡμῶν ἀσθενῶν (6)   (construction) _____
2. ἀσεβῶν (6)   (case) _____
3. ἀπέθανεν (6)   (tense) _____
4. ἀποθανεῖται (7)   (tense) _____
5. συνίστησιν (8)   (tense) _____
6. ἁμαρτωλῶν ὄντων ἡμῶν (8) (construction) _____
7. ἀπέθανεν (8)   (tense) _____
8. δικαιωθέντες (9)   (function) _____
9. αἵματι (9)   (case) _____
10. κατηλλάγημεν (10)   (tense) _____
11. ζωῇ (10)   (case) _____
12. <u>καυχώμενοι</u> (11)   <u>Independent participle</u>
13. καταλλαγὴν (11)   (case) _____
14. ἐλάβομεν (11)   (tense) _____

Diagramming—Rom. 5:6–8 (grammatical and semantic)

Vocabulary—

Romans 8:1–6

Syntax

1. κατάκριμα (1)   (case) _____
2. τοῖς (1)   (function) _____
                      (case) _____
3. πνεύματος (2)   (case) _____
4. ζωῆς (2)   (case) _____
5. ἠλευθέρωσέν (2)   (tense) _____
6. σαρκός (3)   (case) _____
7. πέμψας (3)   (function) _____
8. first ἁμαρτίας (3) (case) _____
9. second ἁμαρτίας (3) (case) _____
10. περιπατοῦσιν (4)   (function) _____
11. first οἱ (5)   (function) _____
12. φρονοῦσιν (5)   (tense) _____
13. πνεύματος (6)   (case) _____

Diagramming—Rom. 8:1–4 (grammatical and semantic)

Vocabulary—

Romans 8:7–11

Syntax

1. θεόν (7)   (case) _____

2. ὑποτάσσεται (7)   (tense) _____

2. θεῷ (8)   (case) _____

3. ἀρέσαι (8)   (function) _____

4. εἰ ..., ... (9)   (construction) _____

5. <u>αὐτοῦ</u> (9)   <u>Genitive of possession or relationship</u>

6. νεκρὸν (10)   (function) _____

7. ἁμαρτίαν (10)   (case) _____

8. ζωὴ (10)   (case) _____

9. ἐγείραντος (11)   (function) _____

10. νεκρῶν (11)   (case) _____

11. καὶ (11)   (function) _____

12. τοῦ (11)   (function) _____

13. ἐνοικοῦντος (11) (function) _____

Diagramming—Rom. 8:9–11 (grammatical and semantic)

Vocabulary—

Romans 8:12–17

Syntax

1. σαρκὶ (12)   (case) _____

2. τοῦ ... ζῆν (12)   (function) _____

3. ἀποθνῄσκειν (13)   (function) _____

4. ζήσεσθε (13)   (tense) _____

5. πνεύματι (14)   (case) _____

6. first ἐλάβετε (15)   (tense) _____

7. φόβον (15)   (case) _____

8. Αββα (15)   (case) _____

9. αὐτὸ (16)   (function) _____

10. πνεύματι (16)   (case) _____

11. Χριστοῦ (17)   (case) _____

12. συνδοξασθῶμεν (17) (mood) _____

Diagramming—Rom. 8:12–14 (grammatical and semantic)

Vocabulary—

JAMES 1:1–4

James 1:1–4

Syntax

1. second ταῖς (1)	(function)	_____
2. χαίρειν (1)	(function)	_____
3. ἡγήσασθε (2)	(tense)	_____
4. περιπέσητε (2)	(mood)	_____
5. γινώσκοντες (3)	(function)	_____
6. ὅτι clause (3)	(function)	_____
7. κατεργάζεται (3)	(tense)	_____
8. ἐχέτω (4)	(mood)	_____
9. ἦτε (4)	(mood)	_____
10. τέλειοι (4)	(function)	_____
11. λειπόμενοι (4)	(function)	_____

Diagramming—James 1:2–4 (grammatical and semantic)

Vocabulary—

James 1:5–8

Syntax

1. Εἰ ... , ... (5)   (construction) _____

2. τις (5)   (function) _____

3. λείπεται (5)   (tense) _____

4. αἰτείτω (5)   (mood) _____

5. διδόντος (5)   (function) _____

6. αἰτείτω (6)   (mood) _____

7. πίστει (6)   (case) _____

8. second διακρινόμενος (6)   (function) _____

9. ἀνεμιζομένῳ (6)   (function) _____

10. οἰέσθω (7)   (mood) _____

11. κυρίου (7)   (case) _____

12. ὁδοῖς (8)   (case) _____

Diagramming—James 1:5–8 (grammatical and semantic)

Vocabulary—

James 1:9–12

Syntax

1. Καυχάσθω (9)   (mood) _____
2. ὕψει (9)   (case) _____
3. πλούσιος (10)   (function) _____
4. παρελεύσεται (10)   (tense) _____
5. ἀνέτειλεν (11)   (tense) _____
6. ἀπώλετο (11)   (tense) _____
7. πορείαις (11)   (case) _____
8. μαρανθήσεται (11)   (tense) _____
9. Μακάριος (12)   (function) _____
10. γενόμενος (12)   (function) _____
11. ζωῆς (12)   (case) _____
12. ἐπηγγείλατο (12)   (tense) _____

Diagramming—James 1:9–11 (grammatical and semantic)

Vocabulary—

James 1:13–21

Syntax

1. θεοῦ (13)   (case) _____
2. κακῶν (13)   (case) _____
3. αὐτὸς (13)   (function) _____
4. ἐξελκόμενος (14)   (function) _____
5. τίκτει (15)   (tense) _____
6. ἀποτελεσθεῖσα (15)   (tense) _____
7. πλανᾶσθε (16)   (mood) _____
8. τροπῆς (17)   (case) _____
9. εἰς τὸ εἶναι (18)   (function) _____
10. ἀπαρχήν (18)   (case) _____
11. εἰς τὸ ἀκοῦσαι (19)   (function) _____
12. ἀποθέμενοι (21)   (function) _____

Diagramming—James 1:13–16 (grammatical and semantic)

Vocabulary—

PHILIPPIANS 1:27–2:13

Philippians 1:27–30

Syntax

1. εὐαγγελίου (27)   (case) _____

2. Χριστοῦ (27)   (case) _____

3. ἐλθὼν … ἰδὼν (27)   (function) _____

4. τὰ (27)   (function) _____

5. πίστει (27)   (case) _____

6. <u>εὐαγγελίου</u> (27)   <u>Genitive of apposition</u>

7. αὐτοῖς (28)   (case) _____

8. θεοῦ (28)   (case) _____

9. first τὸ (29)   (function) _____

10. τὸ … πιστεύειν (29)   (function) _____

11. αὐτοῦ (29)   (case) _____

12. ἔχοντες (30)   (function) _____

Diagramming—Phil. 1.27–30 (grammatical and semantic)

Vocabulary—

Philippians 2:1–4

Syntax

1. Εἴ ..., ... (1)   (construction) _____
2. ἀγάπης (1)   (case) _____
3. πνεύματος (1)   (case) _____
4. πληρώσατε (2)   (mood) _____
5. αὐτὸ (2)   (case) _____
6. φρονῆτε (2)   (mood) _____
7. ἔχοντες (2)   (function) _____
8. σύμψυχοι (2)   (function) _____
9. ἐριθείαν (3)   (case) _____
10. ταπεινοφροσύνῃ (3)   (case) _____
11. ὑπερέχοντας (3)   (function) _____
12. σκοποῦντες (4)   (function) _____

Diagramming—Phil. 2:1–4 (grammatical and semantic)

Vocabulary—

Philippians 2:5–8

Syntax

1. τοῦτο (5)   (case) _____

2. ὑμῖν (5)   (case) _____

3. <u>ὑπάρχων</u> (6)   <u>Participle: adverbial-concessive</u>

4. ἡγήσατο (6)   (tense) _____

5. εἶναι (6)   (function) _____

6. ἁρπαγμὸν ... τὸ εἶναι (6) (case) _____

7. ἐκένωσεν (7)   (tense) _____

8. λαβών (7)   (function) _____

9. σχήματι (7)   (case) _____

10. ἐταπείνωσεν (8)   (tense) _____

11. γενόμενος (8)   (function) _____

12. δὲ (8)   (function) _____

13. σταυροῦ (8)   (case) _____

Diagramming—Phil. 2:5–8 (grammatical and semantic)

Vocabulary—

Philippians 2:9–13

Syntax

1. ὑπερύψωσεν (9)   (tense) _____
2. second ὄνομα (9)   (case) _____
3. ὀνόματι (10)   (case) _____
4. Ἰησοῦ (10)   (case) _____
5. κάμψῃ (10)   (mood) _____
6. ὅτι (11)   (function) _____
7. κύριος (11)   (case) _____
8. Ὥστε (12)   (function) _____
9. φόβου (12)   (case) _____
10. ἐνεργῶν (13)   (function) _____
11. τὸ θέλειν (13)   (function) _____
12. τῆς (13)   (function) _____
13. εὐδοκίας (13)   (case) _____

Diagramming—Phil. 2:9–13 (grammatical and semantic)

Vocabulary—

Section Two

The Exegetical Method

Introduction

The purpose of Section Two is to lead you to incorporate your knowledge of syntax and diagramming into the larger world of New Testament exegesis. Here we introduce a twelve-step method that will take you from the original text all the way to personal application. We begin the process with a step on spiritual preparation and conclude it with a step dealing with crafting an outline to use when communicating the message of the text. The "Exegetical Method at a Glance" is a convenient summary of the much longer "Step-by-Step" section that follows. Many students find the summary helpful after they have worked through the full discussion several times.

We have written *Biblical Greek Exegesis* with our students in mind. Consequently, the approach is targeted for upper-level college students and seminary students. Our only assumption is that you have already taken first-year Greek. We focus on the basics of exegesis and point you to resources for advanced study. In this way, you can continue to use the exegetical method as your knowledge deepens and your skills develop.

At the end of each step in the exegetical process you will find a bibliography of resources pertaining to that step. We have made no attempt to be exhaustive here, but merely to offer you a brief list of works we consider exceptional. The asterisk (*) signals our recommendation that you make a priority of consulting these particular resources. We have not included computer software or Internet resources in the bibliographies because of the rapidly changing nature of these tools. Nevertheless, software such as Gramcord and web sites such as the Perseus Project are invaluable tools for doing exegesis, and we encourage you to take full advantage of them. We simply chose not to list them here.

At the end of the book you will find a complete set of exegetical worksheets. Make multiple copies of these. They provide a convenient place to record your insights and observations through each phase of the exegetical process. Our students find it helpful to keep their worksheets in organized notebooks. That way you can have your own "commentary" on passages and books of the New Testament for further use in the years to come.

Our prayer is that *Biblical Greek Exegesis* will help you understand and apply the message of the New Testament. Let the exegesis begin!

Exegetical Method at a Glance

1. *Spiritual Preparation*—to prepare spiritually to interpret the New Testament

   1.1   Consider the essential prerequisites for understanding and applying the New Testament.
   1.2   Embrace the appropriate attitudes for understanding and applying the New Testament.

2. *General Introduction*—to gain a general understanding of a book as a whole

   2.1   Read through the entire book in a modern English translation or listen to the entire document on tape and record some of your initial observations.
   2.2   Supplement your observations by reading discussions of basic matters of introduction (e.g., authorship, date and place of writing, recipients, occasion, purpose, special emphases, structure).

3. *Literary Context*—to determine how the passage fits into the overall outline of the book

   3.1   Identify the literary type and read a brief discussion on interpreting that kind of literature.
   3.2   Identify the limits of the unit of text you are studying.
   3.3   Discern the unit's role within the larger context.

4. *Provisional Translation*—to render the basic content of the passage in your own language

   4.1   Establish the text of the passage.
   4.2   Parse the key words and make a provisional translation of the passage.

5. *Grammatical Diagram*—to analyze the grammatical structure of the passage

   5.1   Analyze the syntax of the passage.
   5.2   Make a grammatical diagram of the passage.

6. *Semantic Diagram and Provisional Outline*—to analyze the semantic and rhetorical structure of the passage and draw together insights gained up to this point in a provisional outline

   6.1   Make a semantic diagram of the passage.
   6.2   Look for repeated words, transition devices, and parallelism.
   6.3   Construct a provisional outline of the passage.

7. *Word and Concept Analysis*—to clarify the passage by additional study of important terms and concepts

   7.1   Do further reading about how to do word studies properly.
   7.2   Identify and study the words in your passage that need special attention.
   7.3   Investigate the historical-cultural background of concepts that call for further study.

8. ***Broader Biblical and Theological Context***—to understand how the passage as a whole fits into broader biblical and theological contexts

   8.1 Look at the relationships between your passage and parallels in other parts of the New Testament.
   8.2 Look at the relationship between your passage and quotes, allusions, and verbal parallels in the Old Testament.
   8.3 Look at the relationship between your passage and the broader arena of Christian theology.

9. ***Commentaries and Special Studies***—to draw on the experts for additional insights into the passage

   9.1 Consult the leading commentaries on your passage.
   9.2 Consult special studies on your passage.

10. ***Polished Translation and Extended Paraphrase***—to produce a finished translation and to highlight additional insights discovered in the exegetical process

   10.1 Produce a finished translation of your passage.
   10.2 Write an extended paraphrase of your passage.

11. ***Application***—to identify general principles conveyed by the passage and apply them to a modern audience

   11.1 Summarize the original situation or problem.
   11.2 List the general principles communicated by the passage ("boiling down the truth").
   11.3 Observe how the principles in the text address the original situation.
   11.4 Identify a parallel situation in a modern context that contains all the key elements identified in Step 11.3.
   11.5 Identify the various areas of life to which the passage might apply ("slicing up life").
   11.6 Make specific application to the target audience ("primary life applications").

12. ***Preaching/Teaching Outline***—to develop an outline for use in preaching or teaching that is both biblical and relevant

   12.1 Retrieve your provisional outline and revise it based on what you have discovered in Steps 7–11.
   12.2 Craft your outline to a form suitable for communication.
   12.3 Prepare your own heart to preach or teach the biblical message.

Exegetical Method Step by Step

Step 1—Spiritual Preparation

> **Purpose → To prepare spiritually to interpret the New Testament**

Overview of Step 1

1.1— Consider the essential prerequisites for understanding and applying the New Testament
1.2— Embrace the appropriate attitudes for understanding and applying the New Testament

At a recent meeting of biblical scholars, Gordon Fee spoke passionately about the need for exegesis to culminate in worship.[1] The address was so moving that at its conclusion the entire group of scholars stood and sang the doxology. What an experience!

Fee observed that many in academic circles prefer to keep the exegetical task separate from the devotional. He went on to argue (persuasively we think) that a concern for spiritual matters should motivate us to work hard at exegesis, and exegesis should result in a deeper devotion to God (i.e., spirituality → exegesis → spirituality). In fact, a commitment to Christ and the church is vital for the exegetical process since the texts of the New Testament were written originally in a context permeated by those commitments. Therefore, exegesis that culminates in devotion to Christ is the primary purpose of taking up the exegetical task in the first place. Exegesis that does not result in devotion has departed from the original intention of the New Testament authors for their writings.

We approach the task of understanding and applying the New Testament by highlighting a few indispensable prerequisites and attitudes. These are not original with us,[2] and you may want to add others to the list. We encourage you to embrace these as a way of preparing to interpret and to review them in the future. May God bless your work on the text and use it to deepen your devotion to him.

1.1— Consider the essential prerequisites for understanding and applying the New Testament.

a. We need a genuine relationship to God.

This qualification is foundational. Klein, Blomberg, and Hubbard explain why:

> If the Bible is God's revelation to his people, then *the essential qualification for a full understanding of this book is to know the revealing God.* To know God we must have a relationship

---

1. Fee gave the keynote address at the annual meeting of the Institute for Biblical Research in New Orleans, November 1997.
2. We want to acknowledge our dependence on the important chapter entitled "The Interpreter" in William W. Klein, Craig L. Blomberg, and Robert L. Hubbard, *Introduction to Biblical Interpretation* (Dallas: Word, 1993), 81–116.

with him. ... Only the one who believes and trusts in God can truly understand what God has spoken in his Word. This makes sense, for how can one understand a text from the Bible that purports to be a word from God if one denies that there is a God or that the Bible is from God?[3]

That is not to say that an unbeliever cannot understand the Bible. An unbelieving scholar may, through the use of appropriate methods, arrive at what Robert Stein calls a "correct mental grasp" of the meaning of a biblical text.[4] But the person not rightly related to God will reject the value or significance of the text's meaning. Paul says so much in 1 Corinthians 2:14, where he writes, "The man without the Spirit does not accept the things that come from the Spirit of God, for they are foolishness to him" (NIV). Rather than elevate the intellectual ability of believers, the Spirit helps us accept what we understand and act on it, as opposed to rejecting it as foolishness.[5] If the goal of interpretation is devotion and obedience to God, then knowing God is foundational to interpretation.

b. We need a healthy involvement in the believing community, the church.

When we enter into a relationship with Jesus Christ, we become part of his body, the church. But what does being part of the community of faith have to do with interpreting the New Testament? Among other things, being a member of Christ's church expands our perspective, deepens our insight, and provides us with much needed accountability.

Concerning perspective, we need to be reminded that we are not the first ones to struggle with the meaning and application of a particular text. We do not exegete in isolation. Becoming aware of the history of exegesis of our passage roots our interpretation in the wisdom of the ages. Perspective also comes our way when we interact with the views of believers from other parts of the world.

> And since the Church of Jesus Christ is a worldwide fellowship, it crosses all cultural boundaries and parochial interests—a reality we deny if we limit our interpretations and formulations of God's truth to personal attempts to understand Scripture. If we discover the meaning of God's revelation, it will make sense or ring true to others in Christ's worldwide Body when they openly assess the evidence we used to reach our conclusions.[6]

Concerning insight, when we gather with our students to study texts, we have been amazed at how much each individual benefits from the wisdom of the group. As we sit around a table doing exegesis with people who display different personalities, different life experiences, and different gifts from the Spirit, we are consistently enriched by the experience. We prosper from each other's interpretive strengths and gently correct and balance each other's interpretive weaknesses. Studying Scripture within the context of the community of faith serves as a living illustration of the value and wisdom of body life.

---

3. Ibid., 82.

4. Robert H. Stein, *A Basic Guide to Interpreting the Bible: Playing by the Rules* (Grand Rapids: Baker, 1994), 66. See pp. 61–71 for a helpful discussion on the role of the Holy Spirit in biblical interpretation.

5. Klein, Blomberg, and Hubbard are on target when they write, "The difference between the findings of unbelieving versus believing scholars is often one of volition, not cognition. Through their careful work, both may come to the same understanding of a text's *meaning*. But due to their different faith commitments, only the believer can perceive the text's true *significance* and be willing to obey the truth conveyed" (*Introduction to Biblical Interpretation*, 82).

6. Ibid., 86.

Along with perspective and insight, the community of faith offers the interpreter accountability.

> The Church throughout the ages, constituted by the Spirit . . . offers the arena in which we can formulate our interpretation. Such accountability guards against maverick and individualistic interpretations. It provides a check against selfish and self-serving conclusions by those who lack the perspective to see beyond their own circumstances.[7]

We need a check against going our own way. Bruce Shelley asks a question that reveals the value of community when he writes, "What would you think of a man who said that he wanted to be a soldier but insisted that he could be a perfectly good one without joining the army?"[8] Just as the idea of an unattached soldier is nonsense, so is the notion of an unattached interpreter. Even the doctrine of the priesthood of the believer is better described as "priesthood of all believers." For your own spiritual health and the health of those to whom you minister, stay connected to the community of faith!

    c. We need to apply appropriate exegetical methods to the text.

Dependence on the Holy Spirit alone does not guarantee that we will accurately interpret a biblical text. We also have a responsibility to apply reliable principles of exegesis. Why can't believers simply trust God's Spirit to show them the meaning of the Bible apart from interpretive methods? Why do we suggest that those indwelt by the Spirit still need to do solid exegesis?

The main reason we need to use appropriate exegetical methods stems from the fact that God's revelation, though timeless, remains firmly rooted in human history and language. In the case of the New Testament, God chose to speak through human authors who used Greek, with all the grammatical rules it employs. Just as car mechanics need tools that match the part as designed by the manufacturer, so biblical interpreters need exegetical methods that match the means of God's communication. That is not to say that we must rely any less on the Holy Spirit when we do proper exegesis. In fact, we contend that we cooperate with the Spirit more by using exegetical methods that respect the nature of God's original communication than by neglecting such methods.

1.2— *Embrace the appropriate attitudes for understanding and applying the New Testament.*

    a. We need to yield to the authority of the text.

Yielding to the authority of the Bible begins by recognizing Scripture as true and authoritative.[9] But acknowledging the authority of Scripture goes beyond supporting a certain doctrinal position or statement. The attitudes we adopt toward the text in the daily grind of exegetical life speak volumes about our real position on scriptural authority.

Doing New Testament exegesis requires that you spend large amounts of time analyzing specific passages. As the weeks and months go by, you might be tempted to treat the text as little more than an object of critical scrutiny. How do you resist such a temptation? The hours spent laboring *over* the biblical text need to be countered by consciously placing

---

    7. Ibid.

    8. Bruce L. Shelley, *Theology for Ordinary People* (Downers Grove: InterVarsity, 1993), 146.

    9. A number of reliable discussions of the nature of biblical authority are available. See, e.g., the volumes by John H. Woodbridge, ed. *Biblical Authority* (Grand Rapids: Zondervan, 1983) and David S. Dockery, *Christian Scripture: An Evangelical Perspective on Inspiration, Authority and Interpretation* (Nashville: Broadman & Holman, 1995).

ourselves *under* the biblical text. This calls for a prayerful yielding to God in light of the text so that it functions as subject and not merely as object. The Word of God is open to analysis, but this same word also penetrates our innermost being like the sharpest of swords (Heb. 4:12). On a practical level, placing ourselves under the authority of the text means a willingness to be corrected, a willingness to change our minds and alter our views if the text demands it.

Another aspect of yielding to the authority of the text concerns the important issue of preunderstanding. Preunderstanding is a term scholars use to refer to everything the interpreter brings with him or her to the task of interpretation—beliefs, attitudes, assumptions, traditions, experiences, and so forth.[10] You might think of preunderstanding as lenses through which you view the text. Those lenses have been crafted by a number of factors, including your language, family, culture, race, gender, life experiences, and personal background. If you are not careful, your lenses can become mirrors, reflecting your own theological agenda rather than mediating the meaning of the text, causing you to "find" in the text what you actually "put" there.[11] How do we handle preunderstanding in a way that prevents eisegesis and facilitates exegesis?

First, we admit that our preunderstanding exists and influences the way we read the Bible. All of us need to own up to the fact that we bring loads of baggage with us to the exegetical task.

Second, we need to understand our preunderstanding. As we get to know ourselves, we can better pinpoint how our preunderstanding influences certain exegetical decisions. For example, a student whose parents have divorced may, because of the painful experience, develop a tendency to avoid or ignore conflict when it occurs on the pages of the New Testament. Since some conflict does appear in the text (e.g., Jesus' conflict with the Jewish religious leaders or a believer's battle against the powers of evil), understanding this dimension of his or her preunderstanding can only help the student do a better job of exegeting conflict passages.

Finally, we should subject our preunderstanding to the authority of the biblical text and allow the text to shape and mold our preunderstanding. Here you have what many refer to as the "hermeneutical spiral." We come to the text with a preunderstanding. As we yield ourselves to the text in diligent study, the message of the text changes us (along with our preunderstanding). With a new preunderstanding that has been shaped by the text we engage in further study. The result is a spiral of progression conforming us to the message of the biblical text and, because of the nature of Scripture, to the character of God.[12]

b. We need to act on the truth of the text.

John 14:21 sums up the goal of interpretation: "Whoever *has* my commands and *obeys* them, he is the one who loves me." Loving God means wedding obedience to understanding. We interpret not just to understand what the New Testament says and means,

---

10. Klein, Blomberg, and Hubbard, *Introduction to Biblical Interpretation*, 99.

11. B. Keith Putt, "Preunderstanding and the Hermeneutical Spiral," in Corley, Lemke, and Lovejoy, eds. *Biblical Hermeneutics: A Comprehensive Approach to Interpreting Scripture* (Nashville: Broadman & Holman, 1996), 209.

12. For an excellent guide to biblical interpretation based on the premise of the hermeneutical spiral, see Grant R. Osborne, *The Hermeneutical Spiral* (Downers Grove: InterVarsity, 1992).

but also to apply the truths of the text to our lives. Consequently, we need to approach the text with a predetermined willingness to act on what we discover. *Loving* our Lord Jesus Christ means *living out* what we are *learning* from his Word.

Here in Step 1 we have encouraged you to embrace a few important prerequisites and attitudes as part of preparing to interpret the New Testament. These include a genuine relationship with God, a healthy connection to the community of faith, appropriate exegetical methods, a willingness to yield to the authority of the text, and a willingness to act on the truth of the text. We have not listed prayer among the essentials, not because we are neglecting it, but because prayer permeates the entire process as the chief means of embracing the five qualities. As we prepare to interpret—through each phase of the exegetical process and in all that we do—we need to communicate with our Lord.

When you reach Step 12 you will construct an outline to use in communicating the biblical message to other people. You might wish to think of the beginning and concluding phases (Steps 1 and 12) as devotional bookends supporting a small library of interpretive tools. Remember Fee's argument: Spirituality drives us to responsible exegesis; sound exegesis in turn should result in deeper spirituality for ourselves and for those to whom we minister.

On Spirituality and Spiritual Growth

Alexander, Donald L., ed. *Christian Spirituality: Five Views of Sanctification*. Downers Grove: InterVarsity, 1988.

Anderson, Ray S. *Living the Spiritually Balanced Life*. Grand Rapids: Baker, 1998.

Dockery, David S., and David P. Gushee. "Spirituality and Spiritual Growth." Pp. 81–93 in *Preparing for Christian Ministry: An Evangelical Approach*. Ed. David P. Gushee and Walter C. Jackson. Wheaton: Victor Books, 1996.

Foster, Richard J. *Celebration of Discipline*. 20th Anniversary Edition. San Francisco: HarperCollins, 1998.

Lovelace, Richard. *Dynamics of Spiritual Life*. Downers Grove: InterVarsity, 1979.

McGrath, Alister E. *Beyond the Quiet Time: Practical Evangelical Spirituality*. Grand Rapids: Baker, 1996.

_____. *Spirituality in an Age of Change: Rediscovering the Spirit of the Reformers*. Grand Rapids: Zondervan, 1994.

Mulholland, M. Robert, Jr. *Invitation to a Journey: A Road Map for Spiritual Formation*. Downers Grove: InterVarsity, 1993.

Packer, James I. "An Introduction to Systematic Spirituality." *Crux* 26 (March 1990): 2–8.

Peterson, Eugene H. *A Long Obedience in the Same Direction: Discipleship in an Instant Society*. Downers Grove: InterVarsity, 1980.

_____. *Subversive Spirituality*. Grand Rapids: Eerdmans, 1997.

Whitney, Donald S. *Spiritual Disciplines for the Christian Life*. Colorado Springs: NavPress, 1991.

Willard Dallas. *The Spirit of the Disciplines*. San Francisco: Harper, 1988.

Step 2—General Introduction

> **Purpose → To gain a general understanding of the book as a whole**

Overview of Step 2

2.1— Read through the entire book in a modern English translation or listen to the entire document on tape and record some of your initial observations.

2.2— Supplement your observations by reading discussions of basic matters of introduction (e.g., authorship, date and place of writing, recipients, occasion, purpose, special emphases, structure).

2.1— *Read through the entire book in a modern English translation or listen to the entire document on tape and record some of your initial observations.*

Think of the book of the Bible containing your passage as a large tract of land you are interested in purchasing. Imagine yourself in a small airplane flying over the area, and consider how a trip of that sort would enhance your perspective, aiding you in making your decision. Reading through the entire book may be compared to a "fly-over," intended to give you a sense of the whole and prepare you to inspect the parts more closely.

The extra time it takes to survey the territory will be well worth it. Not sure? Then try this: The next time you get a very important letter, single out the third paragraph and unleash your entire exegetical arsenal on it. Don't bother with the beginning of the letter and don't waste your time with what comes later, just pour all of your energy into analyzing "your section," the precious third paragraph (undoubtedly the highpoint or centerpiece of the letter). In reality (if you are like most people), when you receive an important letter, you devour it from beginning to end in one sitting—and rightly so. Every book of the New Testament was meant to be read as a whole, and although reading through the entire book may seem like an inconvenience at the time, its importance in the exegetical process can hardly be overstated. As you survey the book that contains your passage, you will gain fresh perspective into its main themes and basic structure, hear its tone, and get a sense for what motivates and drives the author.

We suggest that you put your initial observations to paper. This is not the place to go into great detail or the time to feel pressure to do exhaustive research. Just read until something strikes you as significant and put it down, such as information about the author and his circumstances; his purpose in writing; insights into the situation of the recipients; key persons, places, and events; repeated words or themes; structural patterns; and descriptions of the book's tone.

2.2— *Supplement your observations by reading discussions of basic matters of introduction (e.g., authorship, date and place of writing, recipients, occasion, purpose, special emphases, structure).*

After surveying the big picture, you will be interested to see what scholars have to say about the basic matters of introduction, such as authorship, date and place of writing, recipients, occasion, purpose, special emphases, and structure.

We have found that students usually profit by beginning with summary discussions before moving on to the longer, more technical ones. You might want to start by reading the introduction to the book you are studying in a reliable study Bible (e.g., *The NIV Study Bible* or *The HarperCollins Study Bible*). Then move to discussions in a New Testament survey, a New Testament introduction, or a one-volume commentary (see the bibliography below). As you grow in your exegetical skills, you will want to move to advanced discussions in the best technical commentaries.[13]

New Testament Surveys

Barker, Glenn W., William L. Lane, and J. Ramsey Michaels. *The New Testament Speaks*. New York: Harper & Row, 1969.

Blair, Joe. *Introducing the New Testament*. Nashville: Broadman & Holman, 1994.

Chilton, Bruce. *Beginning New Testament Study*. Grand Rapids: Eerdmans, 1986.

Drane, John W. *Introducing the New Testament*. San Francisco: Harper & Row, 1986.

*Elwell, Walter A., and Robert W. Yarbrough. *Encountering the New Testament: A Historical and Theological Survey*. Grand Rapids: Baker, 1998.

*Gundry, Robert H. *A Survey of the New Testament*. 3d ed. Grand Rapids: Zondervan, 1994.

*Lea, Thomas D. *The New Testament: Its Background and Message*. Nashville: Broadman & Holman, 1996.

Stott, John R. W. *Men With a Message*. Rev. ed. Grand Rapids: Eerdmans, 1995.

Tenney, Merrill C. *New Testament Survey*. Revised by Walter M. Dunnett. Grand Rapids: Eerdmans, 1985.

New Testament Introductions

Brown, Raymond E. *An Introduction to the New Testament*. New York: Doubleday, 1997.

*Carson, D. A., Douglas J. Moo, and Leon Morris. *An Introduction to the New Testament*. Grand Rapids: Zondervan, 1992.

*Guthrie, Donald. *New Testament Introduction*. Rev. ed. Downers Grove: InterVarsity, 1990.

Harrison, E. F. *Introduction to the New Testament*. Grand Rapids: Eerdmans, 1971.

Johnson, Luke Timothy. *The Writings of the New Testament: An Interpretation*. Philadelphia: Fortress, 1986.

Kee, Howard Clark. *Understanding the New Testament*. 5th ed. Englewood Cliffs, N.J.: Prentice-Hall, 1993.

Kümmel, Werner Georg. *Introduction to the New Testament*. Trans. by H. C. Kee. Nashville: Abingdon, 1975.

Martin, Ralph P. *New Testament Foundations: A Guide for Christian Students*. 2 vols. Grand Rapids: Eerdmans, 1975, 1978.

Metzger, Bruce M. *The New Testament: Its Background, Growth, and Content*. Nashville: Abingdon, 1965. Rev. ed., 1983.

Perkins, Pheme. *Reading the New Testament: An Introduction*. Mahwah, N.J.: Paulist, 1978. Rev. ed., 1988.

One-Volume Commentaries

Barker, Kenneth L., and John R. Kohlenberger III, eds. *The Zondervan NIV Bible Commentary*. Volume 2: *New Testament*. Grand Rapids: Zondervan, 1994.

Brown, Raymond E., Joseph A. Fitzmyer, and Roland E. Murphy, eds. *The New Jerome Biblical Commentary*. Englewood Cliffs, N.J.: Prentice-Hall, 1990.

Bruce, F. F., ed. *International Bible Commentary*. Grand Rapids: Zondervan, 1992.

Dockery, David S., ed. *Holman Bible Handbook*. Nashville: Broadman & Holman, 1992.

---

13. See Step 9 for an extensive bibliography on every book of the New Testament.

Elwell, Walter A., ed. *Evangelical Commentary on the Bible*. Grand Rapids: Baker, 1989.

Guthrie, Donald, et al. *The New Eerdmans Bible Commentary*. 3d ed. Grand Rapids: Eerdmans, 1970.

*Keener, Craig. *The IVP Bible Background Commentary: New Testament*. Downers Grove: InterVarsity, 1993.

Mays, James L., ed. *Harper's Bible Commentary*. San Francisco: Harper & Row, 1988.

*Wenham, G. J., J. A. Motyer, D. A. Carson, and R. T. France, eds. *New Bible Commentary*, 4th ed. Downers Grove: InterVarsity, 1995.

Step 3—Literary Context

Overview of Step 3

3.1— Identify the literary type and read a brief discussion on interpreting that kind of literature.

3.2— Identify the limits of the unit of text you are studying.

3.3— Discern the unit's role within the larger context.

3.1— *Identify the literary type and read a brief discussion on interpreting that kind of literature.*

Since it takes extra time to read a chapter or two on how you should approach a certain type of New Testament literature, you need to be convinced that it is a crucial part of the exegetical journey rather than an unnecessary and time-consuming detour. Robert Stein's insightful analogy from the world of sports may help here.

> Think for a moment of a European soccer fan attending his first football and basketball games. In football the offensive and defensive players can use their hands to push their opponents. In basketball and soccer they cannot. In basketball players cannot kick the ball, but they can hold it with their hands. In soccer the reverse is true. In football everyone can hold the ball with their hands but only one person can kick it. In soccer everyone can kick the ball but only one person can hold it. Unless we understand the rules under which the game is played, what is taking place is bound to be misinterpreted.
>
> In a similar way there are different "game" rules involved in interpretation of the different kinds of biblical literature. The author has played his "game" ... under the rules covering the particular literary form he used. Unless we know those rules, we will almost certainly misinterpret his meaning.[14]

Stein's analogy uncovers the chief reason for learning how to read different literary types. As interpreters we must play by the rules governing the literary type, rules assumed by the biblical author when he wrote. If we are ignorant of the rules or decide to play by different ones, we run a much greater risk of misinterpreting the biblical text. Something more than our exegetical reputation is at stake here. Misreading Scripture ultimately hurts people, leading them into spiritual bondage. For that reason, we must learn the interpretive rules and play by them.

Gordon Fee offers a helpful summary of the four basic types of literature contained in the New Testament:[15]

> 1. The *Letters*, for the most part, are comprised of *paragraphs* of argument or exhortation. Here the exegete must learn, above all else, to trace the flow of the writer's argument in order to understand any single sentence or paragraph.

---

14. Stein, *Interpreting the Bible*, 75–76.

15. Gordon D. Fee, *New Testament Exegesis: A Handbook for Students and Pastors*, rev ed. (Louisville: Westminster, 1993), 28–29.

2. The *Gospels* are comprised of *pericopes*, individual units of narrative or teaching, which are of different kinds, have different formal characteristics, and have been set in their present contexts by the Evangelists.

3. *Acts* is basically a series of connected shorter *narratives* that form one entire narrative, interspersed with *speeches*.

4. The book of *Revelation* is basically a series of carefully constructed *visions*, woven together to form a complete apocalyptic narrative.

Each of these four main literary types includes subtypes (e.g., the Gospels include parables). Look to the bibliography below for discussions about how to interpret a particular type or subtype of literature. As you gain insights into the rules by which a biblical author communicated his message, you will be in a better position to interpret the message. As an example, notice how Tom Wright's instruction about the nature of the Gospels sheds light on how we should read a passage from the Gospels.

Example → In his book *The Original Jesus,* Tom Wright observes that the Gospels were written with two equally important purposes: (1) to tell the story of Jesus and (2) to address the Gospel writer's contemporaries. Since the nature of the literary type (in this case a gospel) determines how we should read it, then to read the Gospels as intended we must engage in what Wright calls a *two-eyed reading*, doing our best to answer two questions. First, what does this passage tell us about Jesus? Second, what is the Gospel writer trying to say, through the story about Jesus, to his original audience? Thus, a *two-eyed reading* means reading with these two questions uppermost in mind.[16]

Taking Wright's advice to heart, when reading the Gospels we should look for what a particular passage tells us about Jesus *and* what the Gospel writer might be trying to communicate to his audience through the way he has selected and arranged the material. Seeing what the Gospel writer was trying to say through the story to his first hearers is an important step for discovering the text's contemporary application.

Let us look at how a *two-eyed reading* works in practice. Take the familiar story of Mary and Martha found in Luke 10:38–42. First, the story tells us something about Jesus: He criticizes Martha's judgmental obsession with Mary's inactivity and endorses Mary's decision to spend time with her Lord. Jesus shows by his response to the two sisters that "discipleship sometimes requires that tasks be suspended while fellowship is maintained."[17] That is certainly not all that the passage tells us about Jesus, but you get the idea.

Second, Luke uses the story to send a message to his original readers. Here we must look at the surrounding passages for clues to what Luke is trying to say through the passage under consideration. Darrell Bock shows how Luke uses three stories to teach on a common theme—discipleship:

> This text [Luke 10:38–42] is significant both for where it falls in Luke's argument and for the example Luke uses to make a point about discipleship. It comes in a series of three passages, each of which treats a different key aspect of our relationship to God: how we relate to neighbors (10:25–37), how we engage in dialogue with God (11:1–13), and how we view one another and our time with the Lord (10:38–42).[18]

16. Tom Wright, *The Original Jesus: The Life and Vision of a Revolutionary* (Grand Rapids: Eerdmans, 1996), 105–6.
17. Darrell L. Bock, *The NIV Application Commentary: Luke* (Grand Rapids: Zondervan, 1996), 304.
18. Ibid., 305.

As you read one or two of the discussions on the type of literature under consideration, we encourage you to preserve your research by taking notes. In the future you can refer back to your own notes for a refresher course on how to read a particular kind of New Testament literature. Eventually you will find that dealing with various kinds of literature has become second nature. Now that you have identified the literary type, you are ready to identify the limits of the unit of text you are studying.

3.2— *Identify the limits of the unit of text you are studying.*

By *unit of text* we have in mind a small portion of text held together by a common idea or topic. The biblical authors used these smaller units like building blocks in constructing their books. To comprehend how an author has constructed his discourse, we need to identify the smaller units and recognize their role in the overall scheme of things. This calls for finding out where the unit of text actually starts and stops; that is what we mean by *identifying the limits* of the unit of text.

As you get further into the exegetical process and understand the passage better, you may (and probably will) change your mind about the limits of the unit. At this point you just need to decide a few things to get started. There are at least *three things you can do* that will help you identify the limits of the unit of text.

1. Read the surrounding context yourself and look for shifts or changes that may indicate a transition to another unit of text. Changes in several of the following areas may indicate such a transition: literary type, topic, subject, verbal characteristics (tense, person and number), time, and place.

   Example → In Hebrews 1:5–14 the author argues for the superiority of Jesus, the Son of God, by quoting a string of Old Testament texts. This series of quotations climaxes with the author's quotation of Psalm 110:1. Notice the changes as the author moves from chapter 1 to 2:1–4. He changes from *exposition* (explanation) on the superiority of the Son to *exhortation* (what the readers should do) based on the Son's superiority. The topic taken up in 2:1–4 is "The Necessity of Taking God's Word Seriously." In chapter 1 the author mainly uses the third person singular subject "he" as he writes of God's "speaking" Scripture (i.e., "he says"). In 2:1–4, however, the author focuses attention on the Christian community by using the first person plural "we." Thus we can establish the "limit" of chapter 1 by noting the changes as we move into the second chapter of Hebrews.

2. See how your Greek New Testament divides the text into paragraphs. Take time to learn how to read *the discourse segmentation apparatus* in the UBS[4]. (See pages 39–45 in the introduction to that edition for a clear and handy explanation of how to use the segmentation apparatus.) This particular apparatus will give you a convenient glance at how certain editions of the Greek New Testament and modern language translations have segmented the text. You also might want to check several other modern translations not included in the apparatus (e.g., NASB, NLT).

3. Note how some of the leading commentaries have segmented the text. Most of the better ones will feature a detailed outline near the front of the book, along with an explanation as to why they have segmented the text in a certain way. But be careful at this point. Save reading the entire commentary on your passage for Step 9. We have a good deal of work to do on the passage before we get to that stage.

In making a preliminary decision about the limits of the unit of text using these three guidelines, there will almost always be differences of opinion about exactly where a unit stops and starts. As we said before, your final conclusions should be reserved for later in the process. Even so, this will get you started, pointing you in the right direction.

3.3— *Discern the unit's role within the larger context.*

After you have identified the literary type (Step 3.1) and established the limits of the unit (Step 3.2), you are ready to discover the role the unit plays within the larger context (Step 3.3). No unit of text exists in a vacuum; rather, each plays an important role as it works together with other units in the book. Consequently, Step 3.3 plays a crucial part in the overall exegetical process, for it addresses the question of a unit's purpose.

In Step 3.3 you are trying to pinpoint how the unit (or part) contributes to the whole. How does this one piece fit into the puzzle? What role does it play in the larger scheme of things? How does this particular unit contribute to the author's overall argument? Why does the author include this unit at this point in the book? How does the unit relate to what comes before and what comes after? What would be missed in the author's flow of thought if you were to remove the unit in question from the larger section? Finding answers to these kinds of questions can shed much light on your passage.

Many beginning exegetes are preoccupied with discerning what the author is saying within the unit and are not used to looking for the purpose of the unit itself. These two endeavors, however, are dynamically interwoven. Consider this line of thought: In discovering the literary context you are trying to look beyond what the author is saying to discover what the author is *doing* with what he is saying. There is simply no substitute for struggling to understand the role of the unit within the larger context. It will take time for you to sharpen your skills in this area, but rest assured, you can learn how to pinpoint a unit's role or function with accuracy, and it will be well worth it!

Before we tell you how to determine a unit's role within the larger context, let's use an example to clarify what we mean when we refer to a unit's "role or function."

Example → In his commentary on 1 Corinthians, Craig Blomberg introduces the reader to the literary context of chapter 12 in the following manner. Notice how he sets the stage by pointing out the purpose of chapters 12, 13, and 14 before specifying how the smaller units function within chapter 12. In this section of his commentary Blomberg focuses the reader on what Paul is trying to accomplish with each unit and subunit rather than on what Paul is saying in each unit (i.e., on function more than content).

> The Corinthian services were somewhat chaotic, and the more libertine wing was apparently equating spirituality with the exercise of the more spectacular gifts. Chapter 12 thus insists on the need for diversity of gifts within the unity of the body. Chapter 13 stresses that without love the gifts are worthless. Chapter 14 then focuses on two of the more controversial gifts—prophecy and tongues—telling the Corinthians to prefer the former to the latter because of its more immediate intelligibility (vv. 1–25) and giving guidelines for the use of each so as to promote order in the church (vv. 26–40).

> Within chapter 12, Paul begins with an introduction highlighting the basic criterion for distinguishing the work of the Holy Spirit from that of other spirits (vv. 1–3).

Verses 4–6 then ground the diversity of spiritual gifts within the unity of the triune Godhead. Verses 7–11 offer samples of the diverse gifts, while stressing that each comes from the same sovereign Spirit. Verses 12–26 develop in more detail the metaphor of the body of Christ, while verses 27–31 bring the chapter to a close with a second representative list of gifts which stresses that not one of them is given to all Christians.[19]

With the above example in mind, there are a few specific things you can do to determine the role or function of the unit:

a. Identify the larger section that furnishes the context for your unit. If, for instance, you are studying 1 Corinthians 12:4–6, you would notice that the unit (vv. 4–6) is part of a much larger section—chapters 12–14 (or perhaps much of chapters 11–14). You make this determination by referring back to all that you have learned up to this point (especially your findings from Step 3.2) and by reading the text over and over, asking the question: What is the larger section of context that governs my unit? Up to now we know the unit we are studying (vv. 4–6) and we have identified the larger section of context (chapters 12–14); what comes next?

b. Begin to close the contextual gap between the larger section and the unit. After reading and rereading the larger section, identify the smaller units that comprise that section. The unit of text you are studying should be one of those smaller units. In our example, Blomberg divides 1 Corinthians 12 into the following smaller units: vv. 1–3, 4–6, 7–11, 12–26, and 27–31.

c. Next, spell out in one sentence the purpose or function of each smaller unit. Remember, this is more than simply repeating what the author has said (paraphrasing content). You are trying to describe the role each unit plays within its context. We said earlier that function and content are interrelated. Function is based on content and flows out of content, but describing the function of a unit goes beyond restating the content.

By describing the function of each unit within the larger section—a kind of *paragraph commentary*—you should be able to see the author's flow of thought as never before. Most important, you should have a clear sense of how the unit fits into the whole.

Blomberg explains the role or function of the smaller unit (1 Cor. 12:4–6) when he says: "Verses 4–6 then ground the diversity of spiritual gifts within the unity of the Triune Godhead."[20] This concise statement tells you what the apostle Paul seeks to accomplish in verses 4–6 and gives you a clear picture of how these verses function in his argument.

On Interpreting Different Types of New Testament Literature

Aune, David. *The New Testament in Its Literary Environment.* Philadelphia: Westminster, 1987.
Bailey, James L., and Lyle D. Vander Broek. *Literary Forms in the New Testament.* Louisville: Westminster/John Knox, 1992.
*Blomberg, Craig L. "The Diversity of Literary Genres in the New Testament." Pp. 506–32 in *Introducing New Testament Interpretation*, ed. Scot McKnight. Grand Rapids: Baker, 1989.
Fee, Gordon D. *New Testament Exegesis: A Handbook for Students and Pastors.* Rev. ed. Louisville: Westminster/John Knox, 1993.

---

19. Blomberg, *The NIV Application Commentary: 1 Corinthians* (Grand Rapids: Zondervan, 1994), 242–43.
20. Ibid., 242.

*Fee, Gordon D., and Douglas Stuart. *How to Read the Bible for All Its Worth*. 2d ed. Grand Rapids: Zondervan, 1993.

Hayes, J. H., and C. R. Holladay. *Biblical Exegesis: A Beginner's Handbook*. 2d ed. Atlanta: John Knox, 1987.

Kaiser, Walter C., and Moisés Silva. *An Introduction to Biblical Hermeneutics: The Search for Meaning*. Grand Rapids: Zondervan, 1994.

*Klein, William W., Craig L. Blomberg, and Robert L. Hubbard. *Introduction to Biblical Interpretation*. Dallas: Word, 1993.

*Osborne, Grant. *The Hermeneutical Spiral*. Downers Grove: InterVarsity, 1992.

Ryken, Leland. *How to Read the Bible as Literature*. Grand Rapids: Zondervan, 1984.

_____. *Words of Life: A Literary Introduction to the New Testament*. Grand Rapids: Baker, 1987.

Ryken, Leland, and Tremper Longman III, eds. *A Complete Literary Guide to the Bible*. Grand Rapids: Zondervan, 1993.

*Stein, Robert H. *A Basic Guide to Interpreting the Bible: Playing by the Rules*. Grand Rapids: Baker, 1994.

New Testament Commentaries

See Step 9

Step 4—Provisional Translation

> **Purpose** → **To render the basic content of the passage in your own language**

Overview of Step 4

4.1— Establish the text of the passage.
4.2— Parse the key words and make a provisional translation of the passage.

4.1—Establish the text of the passage.

The task of producing a provisional translation begins with textual criticism, commonly defined as "the art and science of recovering the original text of a document."[21] Textual criticism is necessary because no original texts (autographs) of biblical documents have been discovered and because the handwritten copies (manuscripts) that we do possess differ among themselves. These differences in wording between manuscripts (MSS) are called *textual variants*. Before we can translate from Greek to English we must establish what Greek text needs to be translated. Consequently textual criticism stands as foundational to translation and exegesis.[22]

Despite the specialized nature of the field of textual criticism, you can begin now to take some significant steps toward understanding and making use of the discipline. We recommend the following.

1. It would be well worth your time to read an introductory article or two in order to get a good grasp of the basics of textual criticism. We recommend the ones by Gordon Fee and Michael Holmes.[23] In these articles you can expect to learn more about the history of attempts to recover the original text, the sources available to textual critics, the methods they use (including the commonly accepted criteria for evaluating variants), as well as practical examples of how textual criticism actually works. Your teacher may want you to do additional reading in this area. One of the best full discussions at the introductory level is J. Harold Greenlee's *Introduction to New Testament Textual Criticism*.[24] The standard work on New Testament textual criticism remains Bruce Metzger's *The Text of the New Testament*.[25]

---

21. Michael W. Holmes, "Textual Criticism," in *New Testament Criticism and Interpretation*, ed. David Alan Black and David S. Dockery (Grand Rapids: Zondervan, 1991), 101.

22. To be sure, establishing the text serves as a foundation for exegesis, but exegesis may in certain situations play an important role in resolving textual problems. This is because one criterion textual critics use to evaluate variant readings is termed "intrinsic probability" and deals with what a biblical author is more likely to have written in a given context. Only after doing some exegetical work will we be in a position to make this determination. Thus, textual criticism and exegesis are tightly linked.

23. Gordon D. Fee, "The Textual Criticism of the New Testament," in Frank Gaebelein, ed., *The Expositor's Bible Commentary*, ed. Frank Gaebelein (Grand Rapids: Zondervan, 1979), 1:419–33; Michael W. Holmes, "Textual Criticism," 99–134.

24. J. Harold Greenlee, *Introduction to Textual Criticism*, rev. ed. (Peabody, Mass.: Hendrickson, 1995).

25. Bruce M. Metzger, *The Text of the New Testament: Its Transmission, Corruption, and Restoration*, 3d ed. (New York: Oxford Univ. Press, 1992).

2. Next we suggest that you become familiar with the critical apparatus in your Greek New Testament. Most students will have either the United Bible Societies' *The Greek New Testament*, now in its fourth revised edition (UBS⁴), or Nestle-Aland's *Novum Testamentum Graece*, now in its twenty-seventh edition (N-A²⁷).[26] While both the UBS⁴ and the N-A²⁷ share the same basic Greek text, the textual apparatuses differ considerably and reflect the contrasting purposes that lie behind these two standard critical editions.

> These two editions were originally planned for different purposes, and they differ accordingly. *The Greek New Testament* was designed for translators, and while its critical apparatus is restricted to selected passages, the information on the textual tradition in these passages is as complete as possible. These passages are most often those in which modern translations are found to differ, and translators need to be aware of the reasons for their differences. *Novum Testamentum Graece*, in contrast, seeks to provide the readers with a critical appreciation of the whole textual tradition. Its apparatus is correspondingly more extensive, devoting particular attention to the transmission of the text in the early period. For this purpose, however, exhaustive detail is neither intended nor would it be useful.[27]

We recommend that you use the UBS⁴ to begin the process of learning how to read the critical apparatus. Browse the Introduction to that edition (pp. 1–52) before turning to the passage you are studying. As you look at the page containing your passage, you will see the critical apparatus set below the Greek text. Notice that the apparatus consists of three separate sections: the textual apparatus, the discourse segmentation apparatus, and the cross-reference system. The explanation in the Introduction should enable you to make sense of the abbreviation system used in all three sections even before you understand the significance of all the information. Using the Introduction as a reference, try writing out a full explanation of the critical apparatus for the page containing your particular passage.

3. After reading an introductory article and learning how to make sense of the critical apparatus in your Greek New Testament, note how the experts wrestle with the textual problems in your passage. Chief among these secondary sources is Bruce Metzger's *Textual Commentary*, a uniquely valuable tool that tells you why the editorial committee chose certain variants for inclusion in the text and why they rejected others.[28]

After consulting the *Textual Commentary*, you will be in a position to compare the committee's rationale with arguments presented by other exegetes. You will find access to the text-critical conclusions of other scholars in some of the more advanced commentaries. For example, there is a "Textual Notes" section featured in both the *New International Greek Testament Commentary* and *Word Biblical Commentary* series. While the UBS editorial committee certainly does not have the definitive word on text-critical matters and while modern commentators do not always treat textual problems with reliable precision, these secondary sources remain the most realistic starting point for beginning students when it comes to the discipline of textual criticism.

---

26. Barbara Aland et al, eds., *The Greek New Testament*, 4ᵗʰ rev. ed. (New York: United Bible Societies, 1993), and Eberhard Nestle and Kurt Aland, eds. *Novum Testamentum Graece*, 27ᵗʰ ed. (Stuttgart: Deutsche Bibelgesellschaft, 1993).

27. From p. 45 of the introduction to the *Novum Testamentum Graece*.

28. Bruce M. Metzger, *A Textual Commentary on the Greek New Testament*, 2d ed. (New York: United Bible Societies, 1994).

4. As a final step, we encourage you to learn how to evaluate textual variants on your own. Even if your work only confirms the conclusions of the experts, you will gain a deeper understanding of the issues and perhaps uncover other exegetical insights along the way.

Learning how to do textual criticism for yourself is not something that we can explain adequately in a few paragraphs. Here we refer you to discussions where you can see how textual criticism is practiced. Working through specific New Testament examples will do as much as anything to deepen your understanding and sharpen your skills. We have found the following discussions to be especially helpful: Aland and Aland, *Text of the New Testament*, 275–311; Greenlee, *Introduction to New Testament Textual Criticism*, 111–31; Holmes, "New Testament Textual Criticism," 56–74; "Textual Criticism," 116–23; and Metzger, *Text of the New Testament*, 219–46 (see the bibliography).

4.2— *Parse the key words and make a provisional translation of the passage.*[29]

By this point in your study of Greek you should be familiar with how to parse the words in a passage. You may already be using the exegetical worksheet marked "Parsing" as a regular part of your studies. We have included this worksheet to help you stay organized as you analyze the forms of words (morphology) and to encourage you to preserve your research for future use. You will notice also that there is a "syntax" column in the parsing worksheet, but you may want to wait until Step 5 to fill in this column. In Step 5 you will be analyzing the grammatical structure of your passage (including how words relate to other words) by generating a grammatical diagram. Here in Step 4 you are simply trying to capture the basic content of the passage. We have included the "syntax" column in the parsing worksheet because it's nice to be able to store this kind of information in one place

Make a provisional translation of your passage. In the finished translation that comes later in the exegetical process (Step 10), you can make your final decisions. Here you just want to put together a reliable translation that helps you get acquainted with the basic content of the passage.

It can also be fruitful at this point to compare modern English translations to discover options for translating difficult words and phrases. You may find it convenient to note a few of the better options in these translations along with a few of your own ideas. This also offers a way to detect possible exegetical difficulties. Gordon Fee wisely observes that "whenever translations have truly significant differences between/among them, this is a sure indication that some exegetical difficulty lies behind the differences."[30] And you will want to be alert to these difficulties as you work through subsequent stages of the exegetical process. The example below illustrates how you could note such options.

---

29. In addition to the rich variety of electronic resources to help with parsing and translation, we list four specific kinds of helps in the bibliography. **Reader's Lexicons** are tools that facilitate reading by listing vocabulary definitions in New Testament order. The books listed under **Translation Aids** take you verse by verse through the New Testament, parsing and defining words and explaining basic points of syntax. Under **Morphologies** you can expect resources that will show you exactly how Greek words are formed. We have included a section on **Analytical Lexicons and Parsing Guides**, but we caution you not to rely too heavily on this last set of tools—they can stunt your language growth. Think of them as friends that can quickly turn into enemies. Use them when you think you know how a word should be parsed and want to make sure, or when you have no idea how to parse a difficult word and need help. But again, use them sparingly.

30. *New Testament Exegesis*, 38.

Example → James 1:2:

Consider it all joy		my brothers [NIV]	when you encounter [NASB]	trials of many kinds [NIV]
pure joy [NIV]	Christian friends		fall into	various trials
nothing but joy [NRSV]	brothers and sisters [NRSV]			

You could get carried away here, so keep in mind that you are not trying to prepare a list of how all the major translations render your passage. Such parallels already exist (see *New Testament Parallels* in the bibliography below). As you think of options and as you consult the translations, you merely want to note what you favor as the most likely possibilities. Later in the exegetical process you can return to this provisional translation to circle the option that you decide is the best.

Introductions to New Testament Textual Criticism

Aland, Kurt, and Barbara Aland. *The Text of the New Testament: An Introduction to the Critical Editions and the Theory and Practice of Modern Textual Criticism.* Trans. E. F. Rhodes. Grand Rapids: Eerdmans, 1987.

Black, David Alan. *New Testament Textual Criticism: A Concise Guide.* Grand Rapids: Baker, 1994.

_____. "Textual Criticism of the New Testament." Pp. 396–413 in *Foundations for Biblical Interpretation,* ed. David S. Dockery, Kenneth A. Matthews, and Robert B. Sloan. Nashville: Broadman & Holman, 1994.

Brooks, James A. "An Introduction to Textual Criticism." Pp. 250–62 in *Biblical Hermeneutics: A Comprehensive Introduction to Interpreting Scripture,* ed. Bruce Corley, Steve Lemke, and Grant Lovejoy. Nashville: Broadman & Holman, 1996.

Epp, Eldon J. "Textual Criticism." Pp. 75–126 in *The New Testament and Its Modern Interpreters,* ed. Eldon Jay Epp and George W. MacRae. Atlanta: Scholars, 1989.

Epp, Eldon J., and Gordon D. Fee, eds. *Studies in the Theory and Method of New Testament Textual Criticism.* Grand Rapids: Eerdmans, 1993.

Fee, Gordon D. "Establishing the Text." In *New Testament Exegesis: A Handbook for Students and Pastors.* Rev. ed. Louisville: Westminster/John Knox, 1993.

*_____. "The Textual Criticism of the New Testament." Pp. 419–33 in *The Expositor's Bible Commentary,* ed. F. E. Gaebelein, vol. 1. Grand Rapids: Zondervan, 1979.

Finegan, J. *Encountering New Testament Manuscripts: A Working Introduction to Textual Criticism.* Grand Rapids: Eerdmans, 1974.

*Greenlee, J. Harold. *Introduction to Textual Criticism.* Rev. ed. Peabody, Mass.: Hendrickson, 1995.

_____. *Scribes, Scrolls, and Scripture.* Grand Rapids: Eerdmans, 1985.

*Holmes, Michael W. "New Testament Textual Criticism." Pp. 53–74 in *Introducing New Testament Interpretation,* ed. Scot McKnight. Grand Rapids: Baker, 1989.

*_____. "Textual Criticism." Pp. 99–134 in *New Testament Criticism and Interpretation,* ed. David Alan Black and David S. Dockery. Grand Rapids: Zondervan, 1991.

*Metzger, Bruce M. *A Textual Commentary on the Greek New Testament.* 2d ed. New York: United Bible Societies, 1994.

*_____. *The Text of the New Testament: Its Transmission, Corruption, and Restoration.* 3d ed., enl. New York: Oxford Univ. Press, 1992.

Vaganay, Leon. *An Introduction to New Testament Textual Criticism.* Trans. Jenny Heimerdinger. Cambridge: Cambridge Univ. Press, 1991.

Reader's Lexicons

Kubo, Sakae. *A Reader's Greek-English Lexicon of the New Testament and Beginner's Guide.* Grand Rapids: Zondervan, 1975.

Scott, Bernard Brandon, Margaret Dean, Kristen Sparks, and Frances LaZar. *Reading New Testament Greek: Complete Word Lists and Reader's Guide.* Peabody, Mass.: Hendrickson, 1993.

Translation Aids

Rogers, Cleon L., Jr., and Cleon L. Rogers III. *A New Linguistic and Exegetical Key to the Greek New Testament*. Grand Rapids: Zondervan, forthcoming.

Zerwick, Max, and Mary Grosvenor. *A Grammatical Analysis of the Greek New Testament*. 2 vols. Rome: Biblical Institute Press, 1974, 1979.

Morphologies

Brooks, James A., and Carlton L. Winbery. *A Morphology of New Testament Greek: Review and Reference Grammar*. Lanham, Md.: Univ. Press of America, 1994.

Greenlee, J. Harold. *A New Testament Greek Morpheme Lexicon*. Grand Rapids: Zondervan, 1983.

Mounce, William D. *The Morphology of Biblical Greek*. Grand Rapids: Zondervan, 1994.

Analytical Lexicons and Parsing Guides

Han, Nathan E. *A Parsing Guide to the Greek New Testament*. Scottsdale, Pa.: Herald, 1971.

*Mounce, William D. *The Analytical Lexicon to the Greek New Testament*. Grand Rapids: Zondervan, 1993.

Perschbacher, Wesley J., ed. *The New Analytical Greek Lexicon*. Peabody, Mass.: Hendrickson, 1990.

New Testament Parallels

The Comparative Study Bible. Grand Rapids: Zondervan, 1984.

Eight Translation New Testament. Wheaton: Tyndale, 1974.

*Kohlenberger, John R. III, ed. *The Precise Parallel New Testament*. Oxford: Oxford Univ. Press, 1995.

Vaughan, Curtis, ed. *The Bible From Twenty-Six Translations*. Reprint. Grand Rapids: Baker, 1988.

Step 5—Grammatical Analysis

Purpose → **To examine the grammatical structure of the passage on both the paragraph and sentence levels**

Overview of Step 5

5.1— Analyze the syntax of the passage.
5.2— Make a grammatical diagram of the passage.

5.1— *Analyze the syntax of the passage.*

Now that you have established the text, parsed the key words, and made a provisional translation of your passage, you are ready to analyze its syntactical structure (i.e., to look more closely at relationships within the sentences). Begin by deciding the syntax of the important terms in your passage.[31] We suggest the following:

1. With the parsing worksheet and your provisional translation in front of you, select the terms in your passage that call for syntactical analysis. Making good decisions about which terms deserve analysis is itself a significant exegetical skill, and one that will improve with practice. When in doubt try at least to decide the syntax for the main nouns and verbs.
2. Turn to the indexes in the intermediate and advanced grammars (see the bibliography) and find the verses that contain the terms you have selected. In this way you are working from the New Testament to the grammars, then back to the New Testament. Often as you use the grammar indexes on your passage, you will want to pause and do additional reading to deepen your understanding of a particular point of grammar.
3. Write your conclusions in the syntax column of the parsing worksheet and adjust your provisional translation as needed (see Step 4).

5.2— *Make a grammatical diagram of the passage.*

Now it's time to display the grammatical structure within your passage by means of a diagram. (Here we point you back to the extensive set of instructions on "How to Do Grammatical Diagramming" in Section One of *Biblical Greek Exegesis*.) You may actually prefer to diagram your passage (Step 5.2) in conjunction with your analysis of syntax (Step 5.1). Some students find that doing these two steps simultaneously focuses their efforts and saves them time.

The grammatical diagram will help you see how the words, phrases, clauses, and sentences within your passage relate to each other. Picturing these kinds of relationships can be of enormous help in trying to understand an author's flow of thought and in developing an

---

31. On the value of Greek syntax for New Testament exegesis, see the following: Gordon D. Fee, "The Analysis of Grammar," *New Testament Exegesis*, 92–99; J. Harold Greenlee, "The Importance of Syntax for the Proper Understanding of the Sacred Text of the New Testament," *Evangelical Quarterly* 44 (1972): 131–46; K. L. McKay, "Syntax in Exegesis," *Tyndale Bulletin* 23 (1981): 39–57; Scot McKnight, "New Testament Greek Grammatical Analysis," *Introducing New Testament Interpretation*, ed. Scot McKnight (Grand Rapids: Baker, 1989), 75–95.

outline to use in communicating the meaning of the text. Notice how the grammatical diagram of Romans 8:10 visually portrays the structure of the verse.

Example → Grammatical Diagram of Romans 8:10

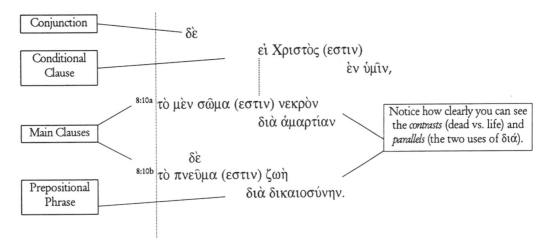

Whether you analyze syntax and do grammatical diagramming as one step or two, your conclusions about syntax should be consistent with what you show in your grammatical diagram. Often the discipline of diagramming itself will encourage you to stay consistent. The grammatical diagram now becomes the basis for the semantic diagram you will construct as a part of Step 6.

Intermediate and Advanced Grammars

*Blass, Friedrich, and Albert Debrunner. *A Greek Grammar of the New Testament and Other Early Christian Literature.* Trans. Robert W. Funk. Chicago: Univ. of Chicago Press, 1961.

*Brooks, James A., and Carlton L. Winbery. *Syntax of New Testament Greek.* Lanham, Md.: Univ. Press of America, 1979.

Burton, Ernest D. *Syntax of Moods and Tenses in New Testament Greek.* 3d ed. Chicago: Univ. of Chicago Press, 1900.

Dana, H. E., and J. R. Mantey. *A Manual Grammar of the Greek New Testament.* New York: Macmillan, 1927.

Greenlee, J. Harold. *A Concise Exegetical Grammar of the New Testament Greek.* Grand Rapids: Eerdmans, 1963.

LaSor, William S. *Handbook of New Testament Greek: An Inductive Approach Based on the Greek Text of Acts.* 2 vols. Grand Rapids: Eerdmans, 1973.

Moule, C. F. D. *An Idiom Book of New Testament Greek.* 2d ed. Cambridge: Cambridge Univ. Press, 1963.

Moulton, James H. *A Grammar of New Testament Greek.* 4 vols. Edinburgh: T. & T. Clark, 1908–1976.

Perschbacher, Wesley J. *New Testament Greek Syntax: An Illustrated Manual.* Chicago: Moody, 1995.

Porter, Stanley E. *Idioms of the Greek New Testament.* 2d ed. Sheffield: JSOT, 1994.

Robertson, A. T. *A Grammar of the Greek New Testament in the Light of Historical Research.* 4th ed. Nashville: Broadman, 1934.

Robertson, A. T., and W. H. Davis. *A New Short Grammar of the Greek Testament.* 10th ed. New York: Harper & Brothers, 1958.

*Wallace, Daniel B. *Greek Grammar Beyond the Basics: An Exegetical Syntax of the New Testament.* Grand Rapids: Zondervan, 1996.

*Young, Richard A. *Intermediate New Testament Greek: A Linguistic and Exegetical Approach.* Nashville: Broadman & Holman, 1994.

Zerwick, Max. *Biblical Greek Illustrated by Examples.* Rome: Biblical Institute Press, 1963.

Special Studies in Greek Grammar

Fanning, Buist. M. *Verbal Aspect in New Testament Greek*. Oxford: Clarendon, 1990.

Harris, Murray J. "Appendix: Prepositions and Theology in New Testament Greek." Pp. 1171–1215 in *New International Dictionary of New Testament Theology*, ed. Colin Brown, vol. 3. Grand Rapids: Zondervan, 1978.

McKay, K. L. *A New Syntax of the Verb in New Testament Greek: An Aspectual Approach*. Studies in Biblical Greek 5. New York: Peter Lang, 1993.

Porter, Stanley E. *Verbal Aspect in the Greek of the New Testament, with Reference to Tense and Mood*. 2d ed. Studies in Biblical Greek 1. New York: Peter Lang, 1993.

Porter, Stanley E., and D. A. Carson. *Biblical Greek Language and Linguistics: Open Questions in Current Research*. JSNTSup 72. Sheffield: JSOT , 1993.

Thrall, Margaret E. *Greek Particles in the New Testament: Linguistic and Exegetical Studies*. New Testament Tools and Studies 3. Leiden: Brill, 1962.

Turner, Nigel. *Grammatical Insights into the New Testament*. Edinburgh: T. & T. Clark, 1965.

Step 6—Semantic Diagram
and Provisional Outline

> **Purpose** → **To analyze the semantic and rhetorical structure of the passage and draw together insights gained up to this point in a provisional outline**

Overview of Step 6

6.1— Make a semantic diagram of the passage.
6.2— Look for repeated words, transition devices, and parallelism.
6.3— Construct a provisional outline of the passage.

6.1— *Make a semantic diagram of the passage.*

Review the instructions on "How to Do Semantic Diagramming" in Section One of *Biblical Greek Exegesis*, where we explain the significance of semantic diagramming and show you how it works. We cannot overemphasize the importance of this phase of the exegetical process! We have found semantic diagramming to be the single most dynamic tool to move students from the nuts and bolts of grammar toward a comprehension of a whole passage's structure and message.

The semantic diagram builds on the grammatical diagram, but the focus here is not on grammar, although there will be overlap with grammar. The whole purpose of semantic diagramming is to help you understand how clauses, sentences, and paragraphs connect to one another in order to convey a message. We do a semantic diagram by drawing lines to the left of the grammatical diagram to show connections that hold texts together. These lines are "tagged" to show the function of each member as it relates to other members in its context. In this way the meaning implicit within the text is made explicit to the interpreter.

We illustrated the process of doing grammatical diagramming using Romans 8:10 in Step 5 above. Now let us return to the same verse and review how we do semantic diagramming.

Example → Semantic Diagram of Romans 8:10

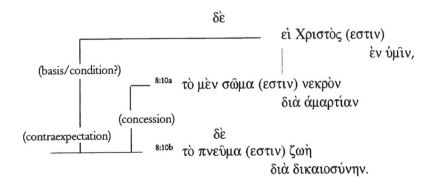

Grammatically, the opening clause (beginning with εἰ) is a conditional clause that qualifies the main clause in 8:10a. But semantically the same opening clause ("if Christ is in you") serves as the basis or foundation for the rest of the verse, especially 8:10b.

Notice that even though the two main clauses are grammatically coordinate, the first is subordinate to the second semantically. That is, the expression "although the body is dead because of sin" is a concession to the contraexpectation—or what one of our students called the "sweet surprise"—that follows: "the Spirit is life because of righteousness."

The semantic diagram helps us understand the verse in this way: "But if Christ is in you—and I, Paul, am assuming that he is—then although the body is dead because of sin (a negative concession we must surely grant), the Spirit is life because of righteousness."

In your struggle to identify the best "tag" for a particular relationship, you are being forced to grapple with text in a meaningful way. Besides offering a stimulating challenge, the discernment of semantic relationships provides a reliable basis for your provisional outline in Step 6.3. Before we move to the outline, we need to say a word about observing rhetorical patterns within the passage.

6.2— *Look for repeated words, transition devices, and parallelism.*

At this point we encourage students to look for rhetorical devices and patterns within the text.[32] First, look for repeated words or phrases and highlight them in the diagram, using different shapes (circles, rectangles, diamonds) or color coding.

Example → In a diagram of Romans 8:9–11 you might circle or underline in red all the occurrences of the word πνεῦμα.

Next, mark transition devices, such as hook words. A hook word transition occurs when an author uses the same word at the end of one unit and the beginning of the next.[33]

Example → In James 1:4 the author says, "And let endurance have its perfect result, that you may be perfect and complete, lacking in nothing" (NASB). In verse 5 he starts a discussion on wisdom, saying, "If any of you lacks wisdom, let him ask of God. . . ." Notice that the word "lack" (λείπω) is used at the end of one unit and the beginning of the next. This stylistic device effects smooth transitions between units.

Finally, look for different types of parallelism, such as inclusio or chiasmus, and mark these out to the right of the diagram. An inclusio occurs when the author closes a unit with a statement that is the same or approximate to the statement with which he opened the unit.[34] A chiasmus is a pattern in the text that also uses distant parallelism. This, however, involves more elements, such as when an A B C C′ B′ A′ pattern occurs in the text.

Example 1 (inclusio) → Look at Hebrews 1:5 and 1:13. These two verses mark the beginning and ending of the unit. In verse 5 the author poses the rhetorical question: "For to which of the angels has he said at any time . . . ?" The author repeats the question with slight variation at the beginning of verse 13.

---

32. For more information on such devices, see the reprint of E. W. Bullinger, *Figures of Speech Used in the Bible* (Grand Rapids: Baker, 1977); or, more recently, David Alan Black, *Linguistics for Students of New Testament Greek*, 2d ed. (Grand Rapids: Baker, 1995), 132–36; Nida et al., *Style and Discourse* (Cape Town, South Africa: Bible Society of South Africa, 1983), 172–91.

33. George H. Guthrie, *The Structure of Hebrews: A Text-Linguistic Analysis*, Supplements to Novum Testamentum (Leiden: E. J. Brill, 1994), 96–100.

34. Guthrie, *The Structure of Hebrews*, 14–15.

Example 2 (chiasmus) → Look at Colossians 1:15–20 in your Greek text. Murray Harris, in his commentary on Colossians, identifies three interlocked instances of chiasmus in this passage.[35] Take a moment and find the uses of ἐν αὐτῷ, δι᾽ αὐτοῦ, τὰ πάντα, and the references to the heavens and earth at the beginning and ending of the passage. Can you figure out the chiasmus pattern?

This completes your analysis of the structure of the passage. You will grow to appreciate being able to map the grammatical, semantic, and literary structure of your passage in one location.

6.3— *Construct a provisional outline of the passage.*

Now it's time in the exegetical process to "come up for air" and construct a provisional outline of your passage, based on your semantic diagram. The focus here is on the meaning of the text (i.e., an exegetical outline) rather than the application for the modern audience (i.e., an expositional outline). You have been immersed in analysis for several steps now, and there is a risk of missing the forest for the trees. Before you get lost in the details of analysis, pause and synthesize your findings in the form of an outline. The exegetical method used in *Biblical Greek Exegesis* involves a movement back and forth between the whole (synthesis) and the parts (analysis). This process of breaking down the passage and putting it back together again enables you to see the meaning of the parts in light of the whole and to gain a new understanding of the whole based on a deeper grasp of the parts. We have found that asking students to create a provisional outline at this point in the process offers them a chance to regroup before going back to analysis.

Some may wonder why we suggest putting together an outline even before doing word studies or reading commentaries. As we mentioned above, there is the need to pause and draw together insights gained up to this point. But we also believe strongly that an exegetical outline should reflect the overall structure of the text more than any one isolated element. Too often outlines narrowly concentrate on significant words and fail to capture the author's overall flow of thought. In simplest terms, we believe that the larger context, rather than single elements within a context, generally provides the most reliable basis for an outline. We also want it to be your outline, drawn from your understanding of the structure of the passage, rather than borrowed wholesale from a commentator. But in the end we do use the label "provisional" and, as with the provisional translation, we encourage you to change it where appropriate as you discover new insights.

Example → Based on the semantic diagram of Romans 8:10 provided above, we might craft the following provisional outline:

1. Since Christ Is in You
2. Although, the Body Dead Because of Sin
3. The Spirit Is Life Through Righteousness

Obviously, this outline is nothing fancy; but it does give a clear summary of the passage based on the structure and semantic relationships in the text.

---

35. Murray J. Harris, *Colossans and Philemon*, Exegetical Guide to the Greek New Testament (Grand Rapids: Eerdmans, 1991), 41–42.

On Semantic Analysis

Beekman, John, John C. Callow, and Michael Kopesec. *The Semantic Structure of Written Communication*. Dallas: Summer Institute of Linguistics, 1981.

Black, David Alan, ed. *Linguistics and New Testament Interpretation: Essays on Discourse Analysis*. Nashville: Broadman & Holman, 1992.

Callow, Kathleen. *Discourse Considerations in Translating the Word of God*. Grand Rapids: Zondervan, 1974.

*Cotterell, Peter, and Max Turner. *Linguistics and Biblical Interpretation*. Downers Grove: Inter-Varsity, 1989.

Levinsohn, Stephen H. *Discourse Features of New Testament Greek: A Coursebook*. Dallas: Summer Institute of Linguistics, 1992.

Longacre, Robert E. *The Grammar of Discourse: Notional and Surface Structures*. New York: Plenum, 1983.

Louw, Johannes P. *The Semantics of New Testament Greek*. Atlanta: Scholars, 1982.

Nida, E. A., J. P. Louw, A. H. Snyman, and J. V. W. Cronje. *Style and Discourse*. Cape Town, South Africa: Bible Society of South Africa, 1983.

Porter, Stanley E., and D. A. Carson, eds. *Discourse Analysis and Other Topics in Biblical Greek*. JSNT Sup 72. Sheffield: Sheffield Academic Press, 1995.

Step 7—Word and Concept Analysis

> **Purpose** → **To clarify the passage by additional study of important terms and concepts**

Overview of Step 7

7.1— Do further reading about how to do word studies properly.

7.2— Identify and study the words in your passage that need special attention.

7.3— Investigate the historical-cultural background of concepts that call for further study.

7.1— *Do further reading about how to do word studies properly.*

If students were asked to vote on the most popular part of the exegetical process, we predict that word studies would finish at or near the top in the balloting. If done properly, the study of individual words can produce a bountiful exegetical harvest. But that qualifier, "if done properly," stands as a much-needed warning that the field of word studies possesses more than its share of land mines.[36] That being the case, we recommend that you become thoroughly acquainted with the proper way to do a word study by reading further on the subject. Try one of the following overview articles:

> Bock, Darrell L. "New Testament Word Analysis." In *Introducing New Testament Interpretation*, ed. Scot McKnight. Grand Rapids: Baker, 1989.
>
> Fee, Gordon D. *New Testament Exegesis.* Rev. ed. Louisville: Westminster/John Knox, 1993. See esp. "The Analysis of Words" on pp. 100–113.
>
> Klein, William W., Craig L. Blomberg, and Robert L. Hubbard. *Introduction to Biblical Interpretation.* Dallas: Word, 1993. See esp. "Steps to Performing Word Studies" on pp. 189–99.
>
> As you move to more advanced reading on the topic, consider the following:
>
> Silva, Moisés. *Biblical Words and Their Meaning: An Introduction to Lexical Semantics.* Rev. ed. Grand Rapids: Zondervan, 1994. See especially pp. 136–69, 201–11.
>
> Louw, Johannes P. *The Semantics of New Testament Greek.* Atlanta: Scholars, 1982.

7.2— *Identify and study the words in your passage that need special attention.*

Now it's time to put into practice what you learned. Turn to your passage and use the guidelines below to help you identify and study the words that need special attention. Here we offer you a summary of the basics of doing a word study, using the tools developed by linguistic experts. As your abilities and interests develop, we fully expect that you will go beyond the basics.

a. Select the words that need further study.

Since you need time to do word studies properly and since time is a precious commodity, choose carefully the words you think need additional attention. You cannot (and do

---

36. For a straightforward treatment of sixteen of the most common pitfalls, see the chapter on "Word-Study Fallacies" in D. A. Carson, *Exegetical Fallacies*, 2d ed. (Grand Rapids: Baker, 1996), 27–64.

not need to) study every word. Take to heart the instructions by Klein, Blomberg, and Hubbard when considering words to study (emphasis ours):

> How does a student choose words for further study? One category includes words the student *does not understand in English*. ... And all interpreters must be careful not to neglect pivotal terms simply because they assume they know their meaning. Words that are *crucial for a passage*, that are *theologically significant*, or upon whose meaning the entire sense of the passage rests warrant careful study. It is better to do a preliminary study of a term and then rule out more exhaustive study than to overlook a term whose meaning makes a crucial impact upon a passage. Study *rare words*—particularly those that occur only once—especially if they might have a major impact on the meaning of a passage. Then, too, a *word that a writer repeats* in a passage is usually significant and worth further study, especially to clarify its function in the passage. The student should take particular care to investigate terms that are *figures of speech* in order to understand the sense implied. *If English translations diverge* on the meaning of a word, the interpreter should investigate to discover the most accurate sense of the word.[37]

This last statement about English translations diverging calls to mind the provisional translation. Remember when you noted the options in your translation in Step 4.2? Your word studies should help you make some of those difficult translation decisions about which option seems best.

b. Study the context that governs the word.

Just in case you missed it somewhere along the way, when doing word studies, there is one rule that supersedes all others: CONTEXT, CONTEXT, CONTEXT! Gordon Fee's remarks are timely:

> In exegesis it is especially important to remember that *words function in a context*. Therefore, although any given word may have a broad or narrow *range of meaning*, the aim of word study in exegesis is to try to understand as precisely as possible what the author was trying to convey by his use of *this* word in this context. Thus, for example, you cannot legitimately do a word study of σάρξ (flesh); you can only do a word study of σάρξ in 1 Cor. 5:5 or in 2 Cor. 5:16, and so on.[38]

That's right, context rules! Now you know why we saved word studies for Step 7. By studying the "big picture" of your passage in Steps 2–6, you have put yourself in the best position possible to a contextually informed word study. Use what you have learned up to this point to influence the decisions you make in your study of words.

c. Discover the word's range of meaning.

Words may have a range of meaning. Just think, for example, of some of the possibilities for the English word "spring"—a season of the year, a coiled device, the act of leaping up, a source of water. The task here is to discover the range of options for the words you have chosen to study. In the next phase you will need to decide which meaning makes the best sense in the context of your passage. The bibliography at the end of Step 7 includes full references for the tools we mention in the next few sections.

---

37. Klein, Blomberg, and Hubbard, *Biblical Interpretation*, 190.
38. Fee, *New Testament Exegesis*, 100.

To determine a word's range of meaning you will need a lexicon (or dictionary) and a concordance. (Remember to use the lexical form, rather than the inflected form you see in the text, when looking up words.) Go first to the concordance to find every occurrence of your word in the New Testament (a service not always provided by the lexicons); then, list each reference along with an English translation of a brief section of text. This may not be feasible or prudent when studying words that are used many times, but when you have time to construct such a list, it will come in handy as you move through the remainder of the process.

As far as concordances go, if you are using the UBS[4] Greek text, we recommend *The Exhaustive Concordance to the Greek New Testament* by Kohlenberger, Goodrick, and Swanson. If you prefer the NIV translation, *The Greek-English Concordance to the New Testament* by the same three authors will serve you well. Here is an example of a list you might construct if you were studying the word σαπρός. (As your facility in Greek improves, the need for a translated list will diminish since the concordance itself provides a Greek version of what you see below.)

Example → σαπρός in the New Testament (using the NASB translation):

- Matt. 7:17—but the **bad** tree bears bad (πονηροὺς) fruit
- Matt. 7:18—nor can a **bad** tree produce good fruit
- Matt. 12:33—or make the tree **bad**, and its fruit **bad**
- Matt. 13:48—and gathered the good *fish* . . . but the **bad** they threw away
- Luke 6:43—there is no good tree which produces **bad** fruit . . . nor a **bad** tree which produces good fruit
- Eph. 4:29—let no **unwholesome** word proceed from your mouth

Move now to the lexicons. With the lexicon you can obtain information about how a particular word has been used throughout its history (word meanings do change over time), how the word is used in literature outside the New Testament during the same general time period, and how the word is used in the New Testament. The standard work here is *A Greek-English Lexicon of the New Testament and Other Early Christian Literature* by Bauer-Arndt-Gingrich-Danker (usually referred to as Bauer or abbreviated as BAGD). The Bauer lexicon, though intimidating at first glance, can become a valuable asset if you take time to learn how to use it.[39] The entry for σαπρός would include the following information.

Example → entry for σαπρός in BAGD

> Looking up the word σαπρός, you will find two meanings listed: (1) lit., of spoiled fish (Matt. 13:48), of decayed trees (Matt. 7:17–18; 12:33; Luke 6:43), of rotten fruits (Matt. 12:33; Luke 6:43), and (2) fig., bad, evil, unwholesome (Eph. 4:29). In addition BAGD includes other references to the term in literature outside the New Testament.[40]

> An important note is in order here. The asterisk (*) at the end of the σαπρός entry in BAGD tells you that it includes all the passages in the New Testament and other early Christian literature that have this word. Since this entry is exhaustive, BAGD in this case doubles as a concordance. Some students will prefer to skip the concordance work mentioned above and move straight to the lexicons. Read on before making your final decision.

---

39. If you have not already done so, it would be well worth your time to read the concise explanation of how to use the Bauer lexicon in Fee, *New Testament Exegesis*, 104–9.

40. BAGD, 742.

You will also profit greatly from the two-volume work, *A Greek-English Lexicon of the New Testament Based on Semantic Domains,* by Louw and Nida. This lexicon arranges the vocabulary of the New Testament not alphabetically by word, but by domains of meaning, called semantic domains. A word with multiple meanings will appear several times throughout the lexicon. Once you locate the domain that contains the word you are studying, you can expect to learn a lot about the domain itself and discover other words that share that domain. Looking up σαπρός in *GELNT* you can expect to find the following:

Example → entry for σαπρός in *GELNT*

> We are told in volume 2 (the index) that σαπρός is included in two domains: 65.28—bad (value), and 20.14—harmful. As you look in volume 1 for the full discussion, you will discover that domain 65.28 pertains to "being of poor or bad quality and hence of little or no value (particularly in reference to plants, either in the sense of seriously diseased or of seedling stock, that is, not budded or grafted)." They list Matt. 7:18 as an example of this meaning, with the added comment that some scholars believe σαπρός refers here to a seedling tree—a tree known for producing tasteless or even bitter fruit. Domain 20.14 pertains "to that which is harmful in view of its being unwholesome and corrupting," and Eph. 4:29 is the only example given here.[41]

In spite of its immense value for exegesis, don't expect the Louw and Nida lexicon to double as a concordance, since they only list New Testament references to illustrate a word's range of meaning. There is no attempt here to be exhaustive. Now you see one reason you might want to do the concordance work as you begin the process of finding a word's range of meaning.

Your work with the concordance and lexicons should leave you with a clear sense of the word's range of meaning. Now it's time to decide which meaning in the range of meanings is most likely in the context of your passage.

d. Determine the most likely meaning within your passage.

From the range of meanings established earlier, select the meaning that fits best in the passage you are studying. Since the single most important factor in making your decision is context, consider the following context-sensitive questions:

- Does the way an author uses the term elsewhere (especially in similar contexts) influence your decision? (Here may be another reason to do the concordance work yourself at the beginning.)

- Which meaning best fits the historical situation of the author and the overall message of the book?

- Which meaning best matches the literary context, particularly the role or function of the unit of text you are studying?

- Do the grammatical and semantic diagrams suggest a meaning that fits the structure and argument better than other meanings?

---

41. *GELNT*, 230, 624.

This raises an important question about the weight we should attach to different levels of context. Consider the following rule of thumb:

> If we visualize the immediate context (verbal *or* nonverbal) as a small circle within a larger one (say, a whole chapter), both within a still larger circle (say, the whole book), and so on, which circle should receive priority? Without suggesting that we can come up with immutable laws to be applied mechanically, one must recognize that the smaller the circle, the more likely it is to affect the disputed passage.[42]

What practical advice! Consider how this might apply to our word σαπρός in the context of Ephesians 4:29.

Example → The meaning of σαπρός in Ephesians 4:29:

> If you happen to be studying the word σαπρός in the context of Ephesians 4:29, you can see clearly how the immediate circle of context should have priority. When trying to pinpoint the meaning of σαπρός in this verse, the strong contrast within the verse (unwholesome words vs. words that edify and give grace) should take precedence over the literal meaning in the metaphors and parables of Jesus—rotten or bad fish, fruit, and trees.

> Practically speaking, when teaching this passage you would want to define an unwholesome word not in terms of rotten fruit (although that might serve as an appropriate illustration) but in terms of words that tear down people and rob them of God's grace. More than just being *bad* or *rotten* words, in Ephesians 4:29 unwholesome words are words that hurt people and destroy relationships.

To sum up, the general rule is that when trying to determine the most likely meaning of a word in your passage, give priority to the smaller circles of context without ignoring the larger circles.

As one last part of Step 7.2, we encourage you to check your work against the conclusions in the standard theological dictionaries (see the bibliography).

7.3— *Investigate the historical-cultural background of concepts that call for further study.*

Sometimes texts include broader concepts that need further study, concepts that often slip through the exegetical cracks. They may be too specific to include in the general overview of historical context in Step 2 or too broad to study as words in Step 7.2. This is the place to investigate the historical-cultural background of such concepts. For example, you need to know something about the structure of the first-century household when interpreting portions of Ephesians 5–6, have some awareness of the financial situation of the person most likely to hear Jesus' teaching on worry in Matthew 6:25–34, and be familiar with the Sophistic movement to grasp the full significance of 1 Corinthians 2.

After finishing the word studies in Step 7.2, look to see if your passage contains broader concepts that need more attention. The focus here is on historical and cultural background, not on theology (reserved for Step 8). One of the best places to begin is with Craig Keener's *Bible Background Commentary*, where he offers insightful comments on the cultural background

---

42. Moisés Silva, *Biblical Words and Their Meaning: An Introduction to Lexical Semantics* (Grand Rapids: Zondervan, 1994), 156. Silva himself stresses that this is only a rule of thumb and not one that should prevent us from appealing to broader contexts (themselves circles of context).

for every verse in the New Testament.[43] In addition, you can count on Keener to alert you to important background concepts that you might overlook.

After identifying the concepts you want to investigate and after reading Keener, we suggest you consult the sources on historical-cultural background listed in the bibliography along with the standard Bible dictionaries and encyclopedias, where you will find a wealth of information.

Concordance

Bachmann, H., and H. Slaby, eds. *Computer Concordance to the Novum Testamentum Graece.* New York: de Gruyter, 1985.

*Kohlenberger, John R. III, Edward W. Goodrick, and James A. Swanson. *The Exhaustive Concordance to the Greek New Testament.* Grand Rapids: Zondervan, 1995.

*_____. *The Greek-English Concordance to the New Testament.* Grand Rapids: Zondervan, 1997.

Lexicons

Alsop, John R. *An Index to the Revised Bauer-Arndt-Gingrich Greek Lexicon.* 2d ed. Grand Rapids: Zondervan, 1981.

Bauer, Walter., ed. *A Greek-English Lexicon of the New Testament and Other Early Christian Literature.* 2d ed. Trans. William F. Arndt and F. W. Gingrich. Rev. and augmented. F. W. Gingrich and F. W. Danker. Chicago: Univ. of Chicago Press, 1979.

Louw, Johannes P., and Eugene A. Nida. *Greek-English Lexicon of the New Testament Based on Semantic Domains.* 2d ed. 2 vols. New York: United Bible Societies, 1989.

Theological Dictionaries

*Balz, Horst, and Gerhard Schneider, eds. *Exegetical Dictionary of the New Testament.* 3 vols. Grand Rapids: Eerdmans, 1990–1993.

Brown, Colin, ed. *The New International Dictionary of New Testament Theology.* 4 vols. Grand Rapids: Zondervan, 1975–1986.

Kittel, Gerhard, and Gerhard Friedrich, eds. *Theological Dictionary of the New Testament.* Trans. and ed. Geoffrey W. Bromiley. 10 vols. Grand Rapids: Eerdmans, 1964–1976.

_____. *Theological Dictionary of the New Testament.* Abridged in 1 vol. by Geoffrey W. Bromiley. Grand Rapids: Eerdmans, 1985.

*Spicq, Ceslas. *Theological Lexicon of the New Testament.* Trans. James D. Ernest. Peabody, Mass.: Hendrickson, 1995.

Historical-Cultural Background

Barrett, C. K. *The New Testament Background: Selected Documents.* Rev. ed. New York: Harper, 1989.

Bruce, F. F. *New Testament History.* New York: Doubleday, 1971.

*Ferguson, Everett. *Backgrounds of Early Christianity.* 2d ed. Grand Rapids: Eerdmans, 1993.

Jeremias, J. *Jerusalem in the Time of Jesus.* Trans. F. H. Cave and C. H. Cave. Philadelphia: Fortress, 1969.

Lohse, Eduard. *The New Testament Environment.* Trans. J. E. Steely. Nashville: Abingdon, 1976.

Reicke, Bo. *The New Testament Era: The World of the Bible from 500 B.C. to A.D. 100.* Trans. D. E. Green. Philadelphia: Fortress, 1968.

Safrai, S., and M. Stern, eds. *Compendium Rerum Iudaicarum ad Novum Testamentum.* Assen: Van Gorcum, 1974-.

Schürer, Emil. *The History of the Jewish People in the Age of Jesus Christ (175 B.C.–A.D. 135).* Trans., rev., and ed. G. Vermes, F. Millar, M. Goodman, and M. Black. 3 vols. Edinburgh: T. & T. Clark, 1973–1987.

Tenney, M. *New Testament Times.* Grand Rapids: Eerdmans, 1965.

---

43. Craig Keener, *The IVP Bible Background Commentary: New Testament* (Downers Grove: InterVarsity, 1993).

Bible Dictionaries and Encyclopedias

Achtemeier, P. J., ed. *Harper's Bible Dictionary*. San Francisco: Harper & Row, 1985.

Bromiley, Geoffrey, et al., ed. *The International Standard Bible Encyclopedia*. Rev. ed. 4 vols. Grand Rapids: Eerdmans, 1979–1988.

Cross, F. L. *The Oxford Dictionary of the Christian Church*. 3d ed. Oxford: Oxford Univ. Press, 1997.

Freedman, David Noel, eds. *The Anchor Bible Dictionary*. 6 vols. New York: Doubleday, 1992.

Green, Joel B., and Scot McKnight, eds. *Dictionary of Jesus and the Gospels*. Downers Grove: InterVarsity, 1992.

Hawthorne, Gerald F., and Ralph P. Martin, eds. *Dictionary of Paul and His Letters*. Downers Grove: InterVarsity, 1993.

Marshall, I. Howard, et al., eds. *The New Bible Dictionary*. 3d ed. Downers Grove: InterVarsity, 1997.

Martin, Ralph P., and Peter H. Davids, eds. *Dictionary of the Later New Testament and Its Development*. Downers Grove: InterVarsity, 1997.

Step 8—Broader Biblical and Theological Context

> **Purpose** → **To understand how the passage as a whole fits into broader biblical and theological contexts**

Overview of Step 8

8.1— Look at the relationship between your passage and parallels in other parts of the New Testament.

8.2— Look at the relationship between your passage and quotes, allusions, and verbal parallels in the Old Testament.

8.3— Look at the relationship between your passage and the broader arena of Christian theology.

8.1— *Look at the relationship between your passage and parallels in other parts of the New Testament.*

Analyzing the relationship between your passage and New Testament parallels might seem at first glance to be a repeat of your work in the previous step. You can expect a healthy amount of overlap between parts of the two steps, as Step 8 flows directly out of Step 7, but there is an important difference. When doing concordance work in the word-study section, you were trying to find every occurrence of a specific word in the New Testament. Here you are looking for New Testament parallels to the whole passage, not just a single word in the passage. Concordance work for a single word may fail to uncover other significant New Testament parallels to your passage. In Step 8.1 you are casting a wider net to discover conceptual connections between your passage and other parts of the New Testament, connections that also go beyond the historical-cultural background of particular concepts studied in Step 7.3.

Example → Parallels to Ephesians 4:29 that do not show up in a search for the word σαπρός:

- Matt. 15:11: "What goes into a man's mouth does not make him 'unclean,' but what comes out of his mouth, that is what makes him 'unclean.'"
- Col. 3:8: "But now you must rid yourselves of all such things as these: anger, rage, malice, slander, and filthy language from your lips."
- Jas. 3:10: "Out of the same mouth come praise and cursing. My brothers, this should not be."

Looking at the relationship between your passage and parallels in other parts of the New Testament involves three substeps.

a. Identify New Testament parallels.

Look first in your Greek New Testament for cross-references. The cross-reference system in UBS⁴ appears at the very bottom of each page. Pages 45–46 in the introduction to that edition explains the abbreviations used in the cross-reference system. Keep in mind too that if you are studying a text in the Gospels, parallel passages are noted in UBS⁴ just below the section headings rather than in the cross-reference section. If you look up Ephesians 4:29a in UBS⁴ you will see Ephesians 5:4 and Colossians 3:8 cited as parallels.

Since the two standard editions of the Greek New Testament do not share the same cross-referencing system, you may also want to look in the inner and outer margins of N-A²⁷. The five to ten minutes it takes to read pages 76–79 in the introduction to that edition will be well worth your time as you try to make sense of the margin notes. For instance, notice the significance of the exclamation point (!) in that abbreviation system. For Ephesians 4:29a, the outer margin of N-A²⁷ gives Matthew 15:11 and James. 3:10 as parallels.

In addition to your Greek New Testament, there are other valuable tools available for finding New Testament parallels. Don't forget to check an English study Bible where you can expect to find cross-references and parallels. Looking in *The NIV Study Bible* you will find Matthew 12:36; Ephesians 5:4; and Colossians 3:8 listed as parallels for Ephesians 4:29a. Also, when working on a passage in the Gospels, be sure to consult a gospel synopsis (see the bibliography). For help finding parallels to passages in the letters of Paul, *Pauline Parallels* by Francis and Sampley should prove useful.⁴⁴

b. Examine the parallels within their own contexts.

Don't get carried away here and spend too much time on this phase, but you need to know a little more about each of the New Testament parallels you have identified. You don't know at this point what kind of impact each parallel may have on the exegesis of your passage or even whether every parallel is a true parallel. Sometimes on closer examination of the context, you discover that some parallels are more superficial than substantive.

Read the context of each parallel carefully and try to understand what it means. A quick glance at a good commentary can help a lot here.

Example → Notes from reading the parallels in their contexts:

- *Matthew 12:36*—This verse occurs in a context of the Pharisees' accusing Jesus of driving out demons by the power of the devil (Matt. 12:22–37). Jesus responds by saying that he believes his accusers represent the bad tree with its bad fruit. Jesus associates the bad fruit with evil speech (vv. 33–37). Words reveal the true condition of a person's heart and as such are directly related to the future judgment of God.
- *Matthew 15:11*—This parallel occurs in the context of Matthew 15:1–20, in a controversy between Jesus and the Jewish religious leaders over traditions about washing hands. The Pharisees and scribes accuse Jesus of disregarding such laws. Jesus responds with a question of his own about why they allow these kinds of religious traditions to undermine the more fundamental commandments of God. He then teaches the crowd that what defiles a person is not related to what you put in your mouth (i.e., food) but to what comes out of your mouth (i.e., words that reveal the heart).
- *Colossians 3:8*—In the context of Colossians 3:5–11 Paul commands believers to get rid of old patterns of behavior that contradict their new identity in Christ. Included among these are evil habits of speech (described in vv. 8–9). A believer's new relationship with God makes certain kinds of speech toward other believers off limits.

44. Fred O. Francis and J. Paul Sampley, *Pauline Parallels*, 2d ed. (Philadelphia: Fortress, 1984).

- *Ephesians 5:4*—This verse occurs in the context of Ephesians 5:3–14, where Christians are told to live as children of light and avoid sexual sins, greed, sins of speech, and idolatry—all sins strongly associated with the world. Verse 4 includes three categories of speech sins: obscenity, foolish talk, and coarse joking. Clearly Paul is telling believers to avoid the indecent and shameful talk common to a pagan lifestyle.

- *James 3:10*—This verse finds its place in James 3:1–12, where James stresses the harmful effects of uncontrolled speech. Since 4:11–12 and 3:1–12 both warn against the sin of critical speech, the larger context of 3:1–4:12 stands unified by a single theme: the problem of conflict within the Christian community. In 3:10 James's phrase "out of the mouth come" seems to reflect Jesus' teachings (cf. Matt. 12:36; 15:11). While warning against inconsistent and judgmental speech, James implies that members of the community should speak words consistent with their relationship to God.

c. Determine how the parallel passages impact your understanding of the passage you are studying.

After you have gained an idea of how the parallels are used in their contexts, you are ready to determine their impact on your passage. We have no magical set rules for making this determination. All we can suggest is that you exercise a large measure of interpretive wisdom. Pay attention to context and don't force a parallel to carry a disproportionate amount of weight. Keep your purpose in view: You are trying to see how your passage as a whole fits into the broader biblical context. Perhaps an example will give you some idea of how to proceed.

Example → The impact of parallels on Ephesians 4:29:

The fact that Ephesians 4:29a and Matthew 15:11 share a common verb (ἐκπορεύομαι) and prepositional phrase (ἐκ τοῦ στόματος) may reflect Paul's indebtedness to Jesus' teaching that words reveal the condition of a person's heart. But the difference in context—Jesus' debate with the Jewish religious leaders as opposed to Paul's instructions to Christians—cautions us not to push that parallel much further. James, who also echoes the teachings of Jesus, helps us see that critical speech can damage a Christian community, a truth that appears close to Paul's concern in Ephesians 4:29.

The parallels in Colossians 3:8 and Ephesians 5:4 catch our eye because they occur in the smaller circles of context. Colossians 3:8 shows that people whose hearts have been changed by Christ should exhibit new behavior, including new habits of speech, especially in relationship to one another. When Paul prohibits the three categories of evil speech in Ephesians 5:4—obscenity, foolish talk, and coarse joking—he may be further defining what he meant by *unwholesome talk* in 4:29. But the immediate context of 4:29—the contrast between speech that builds up and speech that tears down—suggests that here he is referring to speech that damages relationships in the Christian community. This goes beyond obscene speech to destructive speech.

By looking closely at New Testament parallels to Ephesians 4:29 we gain insight into the powerful effects of speech within the Christian community. The parallels in James, Colossians, and Ephesians are especially helpful in this regard.

8.2— *Look at the relationship between your passage and quotes, allusions, and verbal parallels in the Old Testament.*

The Old Testament was the Bible of the early Christian writers. Consequently, the study of how the New Testament writers used the Old Testament constitutes one of the most important, yet complicated and demanding areas of biblical studies. We should point out that the Old Testament appears in the New in a variety of ways: direct quotations, allusions, verbal parallels, and references to persons or events with a specific context in view. In the case of allusions and parallels, the New Testament writer makes reference to the Old Testament, but not in an explicit or direct way. Rather, he points back to the Old Testament by means of a common idea or theme or word. Our suggestions below about determining how the New Testament uses the Old represent a beginning point for further study. We encourage you to consult the bibliography and do additional reading in this fascinating area of the exegetical process.

a. Identify any Old Testament quotes, allusions, or verbal parallels in your passage.

   To see if your passage uses the Old Testament, return again to your Greek New Testament. In UBS[4] direct quotations from the Old Testament are set in bold face type; in N-A[27] they are printed in italics. Also double-check the cross-reference system for links to the Old Testament. Then look in the back of your Greek New Testament. On pages 887–901 of UBS[4] you will find an "Index of Quotations" and an "Index of Allusions and Verbal Parallels." We have found the structuring of the quotation index in New Testament as well as Old Testament order to be an extremely helpful feature. Also check pages 770–806 in N-A[27].

   In addition to consulting your Greek New Testament, use the Hatch and Redpath concordance to the Greek Old Testament (commonly called the Septuagint) to see if important words that occur in your passage also show up in the Old Testament. You could very well discover new points of contact between your passage and the Old Testament that were not included in the listings in your Greek New Testament.

   Finally, consult secondary sources that identify and discuss uses of the Old Testament in the New (see the bibliography). Look especially at the indexes to find references to your passage. For example, in Earle Ellis's work on *Paul's Use of the Old Testament* he includes a wealth of information in the back:

   * list of quotations, allusions, and parallels in the Pauline letters
   * texts of the Old Testament citations (including the Septuagint text and New Testament parallels)
   * list of New Testament passages that combine Old Testament quotations
   * list of parallel quotations (the same Old Testament text quoted at different places in the New Testament)
   * full index of Old and New Testament references discussed in the book.

b. Become familiar with how the Old Testament text is used in its own context.

   Now is the time to become familiar with the various Old Testament texts that are used by your passage. Begin by reading those texts carefully, paying close attention to their contexts. Then consult a good Old Testament commentary to discover more about the texts and how they were understood and used in Judaism. Be alert for insights into how traditional interpretations of the text may have influenced the way the early Christians used them.

c. Determine how the New Testament author uses the Old Testament text.

Since New Testament writers use Old Testament texts in a variety of ways, you need to determine how the author of your passage uses the Old Testament text. Without a doubt this is the crux of Step 8.2. Using what you know about your passage and what you know about the Old Testament text, try to solve the puzzle: In what way is the author using the Old Testament in this New Testament passage? Why would the writer cite the Old Testament at this point in his writing? Does he seem to be using the Old Testament to illustrate a point, explain a position, or support an argument? Or does it function in some other way? If the same Old Testament text is used at other places in the New Testament, do the other passages stress the same themes or function in similar ways?

This completes our attempt to see how our passage as a whole fits into the broader biblical context. Before turning to the commentaries and other secondary literature, we need to take time to see how our passage fits into the broader arena of Christian theology.

8.3— *Look at the relationship between your passage and the broader arena of Christian theology.*

Finding out how your passage fits into the broader arena of Christian theology sounds about as easy as counting all the stars in the sky. And you are right, Step 8.3 could consume a lifetime of study if you let it. But that is not our intention. There is a convenient way of getting a good idea of how your passage fits into the bigger picture: Look in the indexes of major works of theology listed in the bibliography to find discussions relating to your passage, then read them. As you read, remember the key question: What is the broader theological context of which my passage is a part? Let's look at what we might do with Ephesians 4:29.

Example → Two theological discussions including references to Ephesians 4:29. The first is part of the major functions of the church as presented in Millard Erickson's *Christian Theology*:

> The second major function of the church is the edification of believers. Although Jesus laid greater emphasis upon evangelism, the edification of believers is logically prior: Paul repeatedly spoke of the edification of the body. In Ephesians 4:12, for example, he indicates that God has given various gifts to the church "for the equipment of the saints.... " Believers are to grow up into Christ, "from whom the whole body ... "(v. 16). The potential for edification is the criterion by which all activities, including our speech, are to be measured: "Let no evil talk come out of your mouths ..." (v. 29).[45]

From Robert Meye's article on "Spirituality" in *Dictionary of Paul and His Letters*:

> One of the most overlooked emphases in the Pauline letters is his exhortation concerning the spirituality of ordinary human speech. In Ephesians 4:25–5:20 and a parallel passage in Colossians (Col. 3:5–17), we find the strongest possible language—both negative and positive—exhorting believers to give heed to their speech. The Ephesians passage is longer and more detailed: those who have "put on the new nature" (Eph. 4:24; *see* New Nature) are not to lie, but to speak the truth (Eph 4:25); not to employ evil talk, but to use fitting, edifying speech which imparts grace to those who hear (Eph. 4:29).[46]

---

45. Millard J. Erickson, *Christian Theology* (Grand Rapids: Baker, 1983), 1054.
46. Robert P. Meye, "Spirituality," in Gerald Hawthorne, Ralph P. Martin, and Daniel G. Reid, eds. *Dictionary of Paul and His Letters* (Downers Grove: InterVarsity, 1993), 914.

Looking at just these two articles helps us to see that our passage is part of a New Testament emphasis on our responsibilities as members of the Christian community. As new people in Christ, we are to build up each other in a variety of ways, not the least of which is our speech. You will find that your work here in Step 8.3 will make it easier to identify theological principles conveyed by your passage in Step 11.

Gospel Synopses

Aland, Kurt. *Synopsis Quattuor Evangeliorum.* 13ᵗʰ ed. Stuttgart: Deutsche Bibelstiftung, 1985.
_____. *Synopsis of the Four Gospels: Greek-English Edition of the Synopsis Quattuor Evangeliorum.* 6ᵗʰ ed. Stuttgart: United Bible Societies, 1983.
Huck, Albert. *Synopsis of the First Three Gospels.* 13ᵗʰ ed. Revised by Heinrich Greeven. Tübingen: J. C. B. Mohr, 1981.
Swanson, Reuben J. *The Horizontal Line Synopsis of the Gospels.* Pasadena, Cal.: William Carey Library, 1984.

Pauline Parallels

Francis, Fred O., and J. Paul Sampley. *Pauline Parallels.* 2d ed. Philadelphia: Fortress, 1984.

Resources for Finding Old Testament Quotations in the New

Archer, G. L., and G. Chirichigno. *Old Testament Quotations in the New Testament.* Chicago: Moody, 1983.
Bratcher, Robert G., ed. *Old Testament Quotations in the New Testament.* 3d. ed. New York: American Bible Society, 1987.
McLean, Bradley H. *Citations and Allusions to Jewish Scriptures in Early Christian and Jewish Writings Through 180 C.E.* Lewiston, N.Y.: Edwin Mellen, 1992.

Discussions of How the New Testament Uses the Old

Baker, David L. *Two Testaments, One Bible: A Study of the Theological Relationship Between the Old and New Testaments.* 2d ed. Downers Grove: InterVarsity, 1991.
Beale, G. K., ed. *The Right Doctrine From the Wrong Texts?: Essays on the Use of the Old Testament in the New.* Grand Rapids: Baker, 1994.
Bock, Darrell L. "Use of the Old Testament in the New." In *Foundations for Biblical Interpretation: A Complete Library of Tools and Resources,* ed. David S. Dockery, Kenneth A. Matthews, and Robert B. Sloan. Nashville: Broadman & Holman, 1994.
Carson, D. A., and H. G. M. Williamson, eds. *It Is Written: Scripture Citing Scripture: Essays in Honour of Barnabas Lindars.* Cambridge: Cambridge Univ. Press, 1988.
Ellis, E. Earle. "How the New Testament Uses the Old." In *New Testament Interpretation,* ed. I. Howard Marshall. Grand Rapids: Eerdmans, 1978.
_____. *The Old Testament in Early Christianity: Canon and Interpretation in the Light of Modern Research.* Grand Rapids: Baker, 1992.
_____. *Paul's Use of the Old Testament.* Grand Rapids: Eerdmans, 1957; reprint by Baker, 1981.
Evans, Craig A. "The Function of the Old Testament in the New." In *Introducing New Testament Interpretation,* ed. Scot McKnight. Grand Rapids: Baker, 1989.
France, R. T. *Jesus and the Old Testament.* London: Tyndale, 1971.
Guthrie, George H. "Old Testament in Hebrews." Pp. 841–50 in *Dictionary of the Later New Testament and Its Developments,* ed. Ralph P. Martin and Peter H. Davids. Downers Grove: InterVarsity, 1997.
Hays, Richard B. *Echoes of Scripture in the Letters of Paul.* New Haven: Yale Univ. Press, 1989.
Johnson, S. L. *The Old Testament in the New.* Grand Rapids: Zondervan, 1980.
Kaiser, Walter C. Jr. *The Uses of the Old Testament in the New.* Chicago: Moody, 1985.
Longenecker, Richard. *Biblical Exegesis in the Apostolic Period.* Grand Rapids: Eerdmans, 1975.

Silva, Moisés. "The New Testament Use of the Old Testament: Text Form and Authority." In *Scripture and Truth*, ed. D. A. Carson and J. D. Woodbridge. Grand Rapids: Zondervan, 1983.

Snodgrass, Klyne. "The Use of the Old Testament in the New." Pp. 409–34 in *New Testament Criticism and Interpretation*, ed. David Alan Black and David S. Dockery. Grand Rapids: Zondervan, 1991.

For Septuagint Studies

Conybeare, F. C., and St. George Stock. *A Grammar of Septuagint Greek: With Selected Readings, Vocabularies, and Updated Indexes.* Peabody, Mass.: Hendrickson, 1995.

Hatch, Edwin, and Henry A. Redpath. *A Concordance to the Septuagint and Other Greek Versions of the Old Testament (Including the Apocryphal Books).* 2d ed. Grand Rapids: Baker, 1997.

Lust, J., E. Eynikel, and K. Hauspie, eds. *A Greek-English Lexicon of the Septuagint.* 2 vols. Stuttgart: Deutsche Bibelgesellschaft, 1992, 1996.

Rahlfs, A., ed. *Septuaginta.* Stuttgart: Deutsche Bibelgesellschaft, 1935; reprint United Bible Society, 1979.

Taylor, Bernard A. *The Analytical Lexicon to the Septuagint: A Complete Parsing Guide.* Grand Rapids: Zondervan, 1994.

Also consult individual volumes in the *Septuagint and Cognate Studies* series by Scholars Press.

Dictionaries of Theology

Elwell, Walter A., ed. *Evangelical Dictionary of Theology.* Grand Rapids: Baker, 1984.

Green, Joel B., Scot McKnight, and I. Howard Marshall, eds. *Dictionary of Jesus and the Gospels.* Downers Grove: InterVarsity, 1992.

Hawthorne, Gerald F., Ralph P. Martin, and Daniel G. Reid, eds. *Dictionary of Paul and His Letters.* Downers Grove: InterVarsity, 1993.

Martin, Ralph P., and Peter H. Davids, eds. *Dictionary of the Later New Testament and Its Development.* Downers Grove: InterVarsity, 1997.

New Testament Theology

Caird, George B. *New Testament Theology.* Completed and rev. by Lincoln D. Hurst. New York: Oxford Univ. Press, 1996.

Childs, Brevard S. *Biblical Theology of the Old and New Testaments: Theological Reflection on the Christian Bible.* Minneapolis: Augsburg-Fortress, 1993.

Goppelt, Leonhard. *Theology of the New Testament.* 2 vols. Trans. John Alsup. Grand Rapids: Eerdmans, 1981–1982.

Guthrie, Donald. *New Testament Theology.* Downers Grove: InterVarsity, 1981.

Hasel, Gerhard F. *New Testament Theology: Basic Issues in the Current Debate.* Grand Rapids: Eerdmans, 1978.

*Ladd, George. *A Theology of the New Testament.* Rev. ed. Grand Rapids: Eerdmans, 1993.

Morris, Leon. *New Testament Theology.* Grand Rapids: Zondervan, 1986.

Zuck, Roy, and Darrell Bock, eds. *A Biblical Theology of the New Testament.* Chicago: Moody, 1994.

Systematic Theologies

*Erickson, Millard J. *Christian Theology.* Grand Rapids: Baker, 1983.

Garrett, James Leo. *Sytematic Theology.* 2 vols. Grand Rapids: Eerdmans, 1990, 1995.

Grenz, Stanley J. *Theology for the Community of God.* Nashville: Broadman & Holman, 1994.

Grudem, Wayne. *Systematic Theology: An Introduction to Biblical Doctrine.* Grand Rapids: Zondervan, 1994.

Lewis, Gordon R., and Bruce Demarest. *Integrative Theology.* 3 vols. Grand Rapids: Zondervan, 1987–1994.

Pannenberg, Wolfhart. *Systematic Theology.* 3 vols. Grand Rapids: Eerdmans, 1991–1997.

Step 9—Commentaries and Special Studies

> **Purpose → To draw on the experts for additional insights into the passage**

Overview of Step 9

9.1— Consult the leading commentaries on your passage.
9.2— Consult special studies on your passage.

In Step 9 you widen the exegetical circle to see what the experts have to say about your passage. Having done a good bit of exegetical spade work yourself, you are now in a good position not only to learn from established scholars, but also to evaluate their exegesis. Often students are surprised at how much they already know about their passage when they finally turn to the secondary literature. On the other hand, you should not be surprised if, after doing the recommended reading, you feel like you need to adjust your earlier conclusions. We begin with commentaries and move on to special studies.

9.1— *Consult the leading commentaries on your passage.*

Commentaries are books written to explain the meaning of the various books of Scripture.[47] They are valuable tools because they offer easy access to the thoughts and conclusions of skilled interpreters, detailing the possible meanings of a passage and giving reasons why the commentator favors one interpretation over the others. Since good commentaries duplicate much of the exegetical work you are learning to do on your own, you might be tempted to rely too heavily on them. That practice would be analogous to always asking a friend what he or she thinks about an issue before thinking it through yourself first. Commentaries are marvelous tools, and we encourage you to use them, but use them at the proper time—*after* you have done the initial work yourself.[48]

Many students have questions about buying commentaries. We offer the following as practical guidelines for choosing commentaries.

1. Give preference to individual volumes rather than to entire series. As almost everyone will tell you, series are uneven, meaning that some volumes are stronger (or weaker) than others. Even when preferring individual volumes, you may end up

---

47. For additional help on choosing and using New Testament commentaries, see D. A. Carson, *New Testament Commentary Survey*, 4th ed. (Grand Rapids: Baker, 1993); "Commentaries and Their Uses," chapter 15 in Frederick W. Danker, *Multipurpose Tools for Bible Study*, rev. and exp. ed. (Minneapolis: Augsburg-Fortress, 1993); "The Evaluation and Use of Commentaries," appendix in Gordon D. Fee and Douglas Stuart, *How to Read the Bible for All Its Worth*, 2d ed. (Grand Rapids: Zondervan, 1993); and especially Douglas Stuart, *A Guide to Selecting and Using Bible Commentaries* (Dallas: Word, 1990).

48. Every student should read "What Commentaries Are and Are Not" in Douglas Stuart's *Guide to Selecting and Using Commentaries*, 7–21.

owning most or all of an entire series (e.g., The New International Commentary on the New Testament series, edited by Gordon Fee). That in itself will attest to the strength of that particular series. The main advantage of purchasing an entire series is that you will almost always have something handy on any book of the New Testament. We suggest buying a good one-volume commentary to meet that need (e.g., *The New Bible Commentary*).

2. Survey the entire commentary by checking the table of contents, the introduction, the exegetical outline, the layout of the body of the commentary, references to the original languages, notes on text-critical issues, the index, the bibliographies, and so on. By looking through the whole commentary you can quickly get a good feel for the level of detail and the intended audience.

3. Look more closely at the commentary on a small section of text and try to determine how well the writer explains the biblical author's meaning. Douglas Stuart's approach is effective:

> Pick a controversial verse or small unit from a passage—a verse or unit that you know isn't easy to interpret, and skim through what the author says about it. If you are still left with questions, or if the author doesn't treat it at all, you know what kind of depth of discussion the commentary is likely to contain. A good commentary for your purposes is always one that covers the things you are wondering about.[49]

Perhaps the most important thing to look for on closer inspection is whether the commentator evaluates all the possible meanings of the biblical text and provides reasons for his or her own conclusions.[50]

4. Always consult more than one commentary. Here you have what Douglas Stuart calls the "golden rule of commentary use."[51] This amounts to getting a second opinion on what experts have to say about your passage. As you know, additional opinions are necessary because no one is always right. Consulting several commentaries on your passage also gives you the opportunity to read scholars of different theological and ecclesiastical persuasions. As you make your selections, we strongly encourage you to drink deeply from the well of evangelical scholarship now available.

5. Get advice from people you respect. We have compiled for our students a list of what we consider to be the leading commentaries on each book of the New Testament (see below). A couple of disclaimers are in order. First, putting together a list of commentaries does not mean that we necessarily agree with the theological position taken by every commentator. We feel we can profit from a scholar's discussion of the evidence yet disagree with his or her conclusions. Second, since new quality commentaries are published every year, any list of recommended commentaries needs constant updating. We will leave that to you.

What specifically are you looking for as you read the commentaries? Several things. First, because you have already done a good bit of exegetical work yourself, you already know many of the important questions. Look to the commentaries for answers to those important questions. Second, use the commentaries to verify your own conclusions. Finally, glean

---

49. Ibid., 34.
50. A point emphasized by Fee and Stuart, *How the Read the Bible*, 247–48.
51. Stuart, *Guide to Selecting and Using Commentaries*, 20–21.

the commentaries for profound insights into your passage. On a practical level, make sure to check the index in the back of the commentary. The author might discuss your passage in various places throughout the commentary, and you don't want to miss anything.

9.2— *Consult special studies on your passage.*

By *special studies* we mean works that treat topics in your passage but are not normally considered commentaries (e.g., journal articles, essays, monographs).

Examples

- When studying Romans 8 (a passage highlighting the ministry of the Holy Spirit), consult Gordon D. Fee, *God's Empowering Presence: The Holy Spirit in the Letters of Paul* (Peabody, Mass.: Hendrickson, 1994).
- When exegeting 1 Timothy 2:9–15 see Andreas J. Köstenberger, Thomas R. Schreiner, and H. Scott Baldwin, eds., *Women in the Church: A Fresh Analysis of 1 Timothy 2:9–15* (Grand Rapids: Baker, 1995); or Craig Keener, *Paul, Women and Wives* (Peabody, Mass.: Hendrickson, 1992).
- When investigating John 1:1 read Murray J. Harris' *Jesus as God: The New Testament Use of Theos in Reference to Jesus* (Grand Rapids: Baker, 1992).

You discover special studies by looking in the footnotes and bibliographies of the commentaries, by asking your teacher, and by using the standard research tools available in your library.

Matthew

Blomberg, Craig L. *Matthew*. New American Commentary. Nashville: Broadman, 1992.

Carson, D. A. "Matthew." Pp. 3–599 in *Expositor's Bible Commentary*, vol. 8. Grand Rapids: Zondervan, 1984.

Davies, W. D., and Dale Allison. *A Critical and Exegetical Commentary on the Gospel According to St. Matthew*. 2 vols. International Critical Commentary. Edinburgh: T. & T. Clark, 1988–1991.

France, R. T. *The Gospel According to St. Matthew*. Tyndale New Testament Commentaries. Grand Rapids: Eerdmans, 1987.

Hagner, Donald A. *Matthew 1–13*. Word Biblical Commentary. Dallas: Word, 1993.

———. *Matthew 14–28*. Word Biblical Commentary. Dallas: Word, 1993.

Morris, Leon. *The Gospel According to Matthew*. Pillar New Testament Commentary. Grand Rapids: Eerdmans, 1992.

Mark

Garland, David E. *The NIV Application Commentary: Mark*. Grand Rapids: Zondervan, 1996.

Geulich, Robert A. *Mark 1–8:26*. Word Biblical Commentary. Dallas: Word, 1989.

Gundry, Robert H. *Mark: A Commentary on His Apology for the Cross*. Grand Rapids: Eerdmans, 1993.

Hooker, Morna D. *The Gospel According to Saint Mark*. Black's New Testament Commentary. Peabody, Mass.: Hendrickson, 1991.

Lane, William L. *Commentary on the Gospel of Mark*. New International Commentary on the New Testament. Grand Rapids: Eerdmans, 1974.

Mann, C. S. *Mark*. Anchor Bible. New York: Doubleday, 1986.

Luke

Bock, Darrel L. *Luke 1:1–9:50*. Baker Exegetical Commentary on the New Testament. Grand Rapids: Baker, 1994.

_____. *Luke 9:51–24:53*. Baker Exegetical Commentary on the New Testament. Grand Rapids: Baker, 1996.

_____. *The NIV Application Commentary: Luke*. Grand Rapids: Zondervan, 1996.

Evans, Craig A. *Luke*. New International Biblical Commentary. Peabody, Mass.: Hendrickson, 1990.

Fitzmyer, Joseph A. *The Gospel According to Luke*. 2 vols. Anchor Bible. New York: Doubleday, 1981, 1985.

Johnson, Luke T. *Luke*. Sacra Pagina. Wilmington, Del.: Michael Glazier, 1991.

Liefeld, Walter. "Luke." Pp. 797–1059 in *Expositor's Bible Commentary*, vol. 8. Grand Rapids: Zondervan, 1984.

Marshall, I. Howard. *The Gospel of Luke*. New International Greek Testament Commentary. Grand Rapids: Eerdmans, 1978.

Nolland, John. *Luke 1–9:20*. Word Biblical Commentary. Dallas: Word, 1990.

_____. *Luke 9:21–18:34*. Word Biblical Commentary. Dallas: Word, 1993.

_____. *Luke 18:35–24:53*. Word Biblical Commentary. Dallas: Word, 1993.

Stein, Robert A. *Luke*. New American Commentary. Nashville: Broadman, 1992.

John

Barrett, C. K. *The Gospel According to St. John: An Introduction with Commentary and Notes on the Greek Text*. 2d ed. Philadelphia: Westminster, 1978.

Beasley-Murray, George R. *The Gospel of John*. Word Biblical Commentary. Waco, Tex.: Word, 1987.

Brown, Raymond E. *The Gospel According to John: Introduction, Translation and Notes*. 2 vols. Anchor Bible. New York: Doubleday, 1966–1971.

Bruce, F. F. *The Gospel of John*. Grand Rapids: Eerdmans, 1983.

Carson, D. A. *The Gospel According to John*. Pillar New Testament Commentary. Grand Rapids: Eerdmans, 1991.

Morris, Leon. *Commentary on the Gospel of John*. Rev. ed. New International Commentary on the New Testament. Grand Rapids: Eerdmans, 1994.

Acts

Bruce, F. F. *The Acts of the Apostles: The Greek Text with Introduction and Commentary*. 3d ed. Grand Rapids: Eerdmans, 1990.

_____. *Commentary on the Book of Acts*. Rev. ed. New International Commentary on the New Testament. Grand Rapids: Eerdmans, 1988.

Johnson, Luke T. *Acts*. Sacra Pagina. Wilmingotn, Del.: Michael Glazier, 1992.

Larkin, William J., Jr. *Acts*. IVP New Testament Commentary. Downers Grove: InterVarsity, 1995.

Longenecker, Richard N. "Acts." Pp. 207–753 in *Expositor's Bible Commentary*, vol. 9. Grand Rapids: Zondervan, 1981.

Marshall, I. Howard. *The Acts of the Apostles*. Tyndale New Testament Commentaries. Grand Rapids: Eerdmans, 1980.

Polhill, John B. *Acts*. New American Commentary. Nashville: Broadman, 1992.

Stott, John R. W. *The Spirit, the Church, and the World: The Message of Acts*. Downers Grove: InterVarsity, 1990.

Witherington, Ben III. *The Acts of the Apostles: A Socio-Rhetorical Commentary*. Grand Rapids: Eerdmans, 1998.

Romans

Bruce, F. F. *The Letter of Paul to the Romans*. Tyndale New Testament Commentaries. Grand Rapids: Eerdmans, 1985.

Cranfield, C. E. B. *A Critical and Exegetical Commentary on the Epistle to the Romans*. International Critical Commentary. 2 vols. Edinburgh: T. & T. Clark, 1975, 1979.

Dunn, James D. G. *Romans 1–8*. Word Biblical Commentary. Dallas: Word, 1988.

_____. *Romans 9–16*. Word Biblical Commentary. Dallas: Word, 1988.

Fitzmyer, Joseph. *Romans: A New Translation with Introduction and Commentary*. Anchor Bible. New York: Doubleday, 1993.

Käsemann, Ernst. *Commentary on Romans*. Trans. G. W. Bromiley. Grand Rapids: Eerdmans, 1980.

Moo, Douglas J. *The Epistle to the Romans*. New International Commentary on the New Testament. Grand Rapids: Eerdmans, 1996.

Morris, Leon. *The Epistle to the Romans*. Pillar New Testament Commentaries. Grand Rapids: Eerdmans, 1988.

Stott, John R. W. *Romans: God's Good News for the World*. Downers Grove: InterVarsity, 1994.

First Corinthians

Barrett, C. K. *A Commentary to the First Epistle to the Corinthians*. Harper's New Testament Commentaries. New York: Harper, 1968.

Blomberg, Craig L. *The NIV Application Commentary: 1 Corinthians*. Grand Rapids: Zondervan, 1994.

Fee, Gordon D. *The First Epistle to the Corinthians*. New International Commentary on the New Testament. Grand Rapids: Eerdmans, 1987.

Morris, Leon. *The First Epistle of Paul to the Corinthians*. Rev. ed. Tyndale New Testament Commentaries. Grand Rapids: Eerdmans, 1985.

Prior, David. *The Message of 1 Corinthians*. Bible Speaks Today. Downers Grove: InterVarsity, 1985.

Witherington, Ben III. *Conflict and Community in Corinth: A Socio-Rhetorical Commentary*. Grand Rapids: Eerdmans, 1994.

Second Corinthians

Barnett, Paul. *The Second Epistle to the Corinthians*. New International Commentary on the New Testament. Grand Rapids: Eerdmans, 1997.

Belleville, Linda L. *2 Corinthians*. IVP New Testament Commentary. Downers Grove: InterVarsity, 1996.

Furnish, Victor P. *II Corinthians*. Anchor Bible. New York: Doubleday, 1984.

Harris, Murray J. "2 Corinthians." Pp. 301–406 in *Expositor's Bible Commentary*, vol. 10. Grand Rapids: Zondervan, 1976.

Kruse, Colin G. *The Second Epistle of Paul to the Corinthians*. Tyndale New Testament Commentaries. Grand Rapids: Eerdmans, 1987.

Martin, Ralph P. *2 Corinthians*. Word Biblical Commentary. Waco, Tex.: Word, 1986.

Galatians

Betz, H. D. *Galatians: A Commentary on Paul's Letter to the Churches in Galatia*. Hermeneia. Philadelphia: Fortress, 1979.

Bruce, F. F. *The Epistle to the Galatians*. New International Greek Testament Commentary. Grand Rapids: Eerdmans, 1982.

Burton, E. de Witt. *A Critical and Exegetical Commentary on the Epistle to the Galatians*. International Critical Commentary. Edinburgh: T. & T. Clark, 1921.

Fung, R. Y. K. *The Epistle to the Galatians*. New International Commentary on the New Testament. Grand Rapids: Eerdmans, 1988.

George, Timothy. *Galatians*. New American Commentary. Nashville: Broadman, 1994.

Hansen, G. Walter. *Galatians*. IVP New Testament Commentary. Downers Grove: InterVarsity, 1994.

Longenecker, Richard N. *Galatians*. Word Biblical Commentary. Dallas: Word, 1990.

Matera, Frank J. *Galatians*. Sacra Pagina. Wilmington, Del.: Michael Glazier, 1992.

Ephesians

Barth, Markus. *Ephesians*. 2 vols. Anchor Bible. New York: Doubleday, 1974.

Bruce, F. F. *The Epistles to the Colossians, to Philemon, and to the Ephesians*. New International Commentary on the New Testament. Grand Rapids: Eerdmans, 1984.

Lincoln, Andrew T. *Ephesians*. Word Biblical Commentary. Dallas: Word, 1990.

Schnackenburg, Rudolf. *Ephesians: A Commentary*. Trans. by Helen Heron. Edinburgh: T. & T. Clark, 1991.

Snodgrass, Klyne. *The NIV Application Commentary: Ephesians*. Grand Rapids: Zondervan, 1996.

Stott, John R. W. *The Message of Ephesians*. Bible Speaks Today. Downers Grove: InterVarsity, 1979.

Philippians

Fee, Gordon D. *Philippians*. New International Commentary on the New Testament. Grand Rapids: Eerdmans, 1995.

Hawthorne, Gerald F. *Philippians*. Word Biblical Commentary. Waco, Tex.: Word, 1983.

Martin, Ralph P. *The Epistle of Paul to the Philippians*. Tyndale New Testament Commentaries. Grand Rapids: Eerdmans, 1959.

O'Brien, Peter T. *The Epistle to the Philippians*. New International Greek Testament Commentary. Grand Rapids: Eerdmans, 1991.

Silva, Moisés. *Philippians*. Baker Exegetical Commentary on the New Testament. Grand Rapids: Baker, 1992.

Thielman, Frank. *The NIV Application Commentary: Philippians*. Grand Rapids: Zondervan, 1995.

Colossians and Philemon

Bruce, F. F. *The Epistles to the Colossians, to Philemon, and to the Ephesians*. New International Commentary on the New Testament. Grand Rapids: Eerdmans, 1984.

Garland, David G. *The NIV Application Commentary: Colossians and Philemon*. Grand Rapids: Zondervan, 1998.

Harris, Murray J. *Colossians and Philemon*. Exegetical Guide to the Greek New Testament. Grand Rapids: Eerdmans, 1991.

Lohse, Eduard. *Colossians and Philemon: A Commentary on the Epistles to the Colossians and Philemon*. Trans. by William R. Poehlmann and Robert J. Karris. Hermeneia. Philadelphia: Fortress, 1971.

Martin, Ralph P. *Colossians and Philemon*. New Century Bible. Grand Rapids: Eerdmans, 1974.

O'Brien, Peter T. *Colossians, Philemon*. Word Biblical Commentary. Waco, Tex.: Word, 1982.

Wright, N. T. *The Epistles of Paul to the Colossians and to Philemon*. Tyndale New Testament Commentaries. Grand Rapids: Eerdmans, 1986.

First and Second Thessalonians

Best, Ernst. *A Commentary on the First and Second Epistles to the Thessalonians*. Harper's New Testament Commentaries. New York: Harper & Row, 1972.

Bruce, F. F. *1 and 2 Thessalonians*. Word Biblical Commentary. Waco, Tex.: Word, 1982.

Holmes, Michael W. *The NIV Application Commentary: 1 and 2 Thessalonians*. Grand Rapids: Zondervan, 1998.

Marshall, I. Howard. *1 and 2 Thessalonians*. New Century Bible. Grand Rapids: Eerdmans, 1983.

Morris, Leon. *The First and Second Epistles to the Thessalonians*. Rev. ed. New International Commentary on the New Testament. Grand Rapids: Eerdmans, 1991.

Stott, John R. W. *The Gospel and Time: The Message of 1 and 2 Thessalonians*. Downers Grove: InterVarsity, 1991.

Wanamaker, Charles A. *The Epistles to the Thessalonians*. New International Greek Testament Commentary. Grand Rapids: Eerdmans, 1990.

First and Second Timothy and Titus

Fee, Gordon D. *1 and 2 Timothy, Titus*. New International Biblical Commentary. Peabody, Mass.: Hendrickson, 1988.

Guthrie, Donald. *The Pastoral Epistles*. Rev. ed. Tyndale New Testament Commentaries. Grand Rapids: Eerdmans, 1990.

Kelly, J. N. D. *A Commentary on the Pastoral Epistles*. Harper's New Testament Commentaries. New York: Harper, 1963.

Knight, George. *The Pastoral Epistles*. New International Greek Testament Commentary. Grand Rapids: Eerdmans, 1992.

Lea, Thomas D., and Hayne P. Griffin Jr. *1, 2 Timothy, Titus*. New American Commentary. Nashville: Broadman, 1992.

Mounce, William D. *1 and 2 Timothy, Titus*. Word Biblical Commentary. Dallas: Word, forthcoming.

Hebrews

Attridge, Harold. *To the Hebrews*. Hermeneia. Philadelphia: Fortress, 1989.

Bruce, F. F. *The Epistle to the Hebrews*. New International Commentary on the New Testament. Grand Rapids: Eerdmans, 1964.

Ellingsworth, Paul. *The Epistle to the Hebrews*. New International Greek Testament Commentary. Grand Rapids: Eerdmans, 1993.

Guthrie, Donald. *The Letter to the Hebrews*. Tyndale New Testament Commentaries. Grand Rapids: Eerdmans, 1983.

Guthrie, George H. *The NIV Application Commentary: Hebrews*. Grand Rapids: Zondervan, 1998.

Hughes, Philip E. *A Commentary on the Epistle to the Hebrews*. Grand Rapids: Eerdmans, 1977.

Hagner, Donald A. *Hebrews*. New International Biblical Commentary. Peabody, Mass.: Hendrickson, 1988.

Lane, William L. *Hebrews 1–8*. Word Biblical Commentary. Dallas: Word, 1991.

_____. *Hebrews 9–13*. Word Biblical Commentary. Dallas: Word, 1991.

James

Davids, Peter H. *Commentary on James*. New International Greek Testament Commentary. Grand Rapids: Eerdmans, 1982.

Dibelius, Martin. *James*. Revised by H. Greeven. Hermeneia. Philadelphia: Fortress Press, 1976.

Johnson, Luke Timothy. *The Letter of James*. Anchor Bible. New York: Doubleday, 1995.

Laws, Sophie S. *A Commentary on the Epistle of James*. Harper's New Testament Commentaries. New York: Harper & Row, 1980.

Martin, Ralph P. *James*. Word Biblical Commentary. Waco, Tex.: Word, 1988.

Mitton, C. Leslie. *The Epistle of James*. Grand Rapids: Eerdmans, 1966.

Moo, Douglas J. *The Letter of James*. Tyndale New Testament Commentaries. Grand Rapids: Eerdmans, 1985.

Motyer, J. Alec. *The Message of James*. Bible Speaks Today. Downers Grove: InterVarsity, 1985.

Nystrom, David P. *The NIV Application Commentary: James*. Grand Rapids: Zondervan, 1997.

First and Second Peter and Jude

Bauchham, Richard J. *Jude, 2 Peter*. Word Biblical Commentary. Waco, Tex.: Word, 1983.

Beare, F. W. *The First Epistle of Peter*. 3d ed. Oxford: Blackwell, 1970.

Clowney, Edmund P. *The Message of 1 Peter*. Bible Speaks Today. Downers Grove: InterVarsity, 1989.

Davids, Peter H. *The First Epistle of Peter*. New International Commentary on the New Testament. Grand Rapids: Eerdmans, 1990.

Goppelt, Leonhard. *A Commentary on 1 Peter*. Ed. Ferdinand Hahn. Trans. John E. Alsup. Grand Rapids: Eerdmans, 1993.

Green, Michael. *The Second Epistle General of Peter and the General Epistle of Jude*. Rev. ed. Tyndale New Testament Commentaries. Grand Rapids: Eerdmans, 1987.

Grudem, Wayne A. *The First Epistle of Peter*. Tyndale New Testament Commentaries. Grand Rapids: Eerdmans, 1988.

Kelly, J. N. D. *A Commentary on the Epistles of Peter and Jude*. Harper's New Testament Commentaries. New York: Harper & Row, 1969.

Marshall, I. Howard. *1 Peter*. IVP New Testament Commentary. Downers Grove: InterVarsity, 1990.

Michaels, J. Ramsey. *1 Peter*. Word Biblical Commentary. Waco, Tex.: Word, 1988.
Selwyn, E. G. *The First Epistle of St. Peter*. 2d ed. London: Macmillan, 1947.

First, Second, and Third John

Brown, Raymond E. *The Epistles of John*. Anchor Bible. New York: Doubleday, 1982.
Bruce, F. F. *The Epistles of John*. Grand Rapids: Eerdmans, 1970.
Burge, Gary M. *The NIV Application Commentary: Letters of John*. Grand Rapids: Zondervan, 1996.
Marshall, I. Howard. *The Epistles of John*. New International Commentary on the New Testament. Grand Rapids: Eerdmans, 1978.
Smalley, Stephen S. *1, 2, 3 John*. Word Biblical Commentary. Waco, Tex.: Word, 1984.
Stott, John R. W. *The Epistles of St. John*. Rev. ed. Tyndale New Testament Commentaries. Grand Rapids: Eerdmans, 1988.
Thompson, Marianne Meye. *1–3 John*. IVP New Testament Commentary. Downers Grove: Inter-Varsity, 1992.

Revelation

Beasley-Murray, George R. *The Book of Revelation*. Rev. ed. New Century Bible. Grand Rapids: Eerdmans, 1981.
Caird, George B. *A Commentary on the Revelation of St. John the Divine*. Harper's New Testament Commentaries. New York: Harper & Row, 1966.
Johnson, Alan F. "Revelation." Pp. 399–603 in *Expositor's Bible Commentary*, vol. 12. Grand Rapids: Zondervan, 1981.
Ladd, George E. *A Commentary on the Revelation of St. John*. Grand Rapids: Eerdmans, 1972.
Metzger, Bruce M. *Breaking the Code: Understanding the Book of Revelation*. Nashville: Abingdon, 1996.
Morris, Leon. *The Book of Revelation*. Rev. ed. Tyndale New Testament Commentaries. Grand Rapids: Eerdmans, 1986.
Mounce, Robert H. *The Book of Revelation*. Rev. ed. New International Commentary on the New Testament. Grand Rapids: Eerdmans, 1997.

Step 10—Polished Translation and Extended Paraphrase

> **Purpose → To produce a finished translation and to highlight additional insights discovered in the exegetical process**

Overview of Step 10

10.1— Produce a finished translation of your passage.
10.2— Write an extended paraphrase of your passage.

10.1— *Produce a finished translation of your passage.*

Using what you have learned up to this point, write out a finished translation of the passage. Remember that when you translate, you are trying to convey meaning from one language to another. The diagram below illustrates the basics of the translation process:

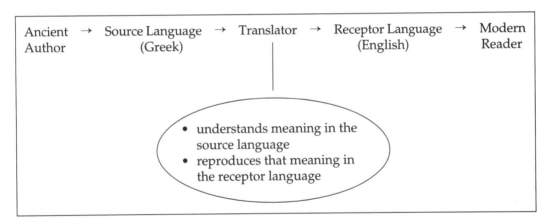

There is no single way of translating, but there are two basic approaches that translators employ, one more tied to the source language and the other more sensitive to the receptor language. The *formal equivalence (or word-for-word) approach* tries to stay as close as possible to the exact wording and linguistic patterns in the original text. According to this theory, reproducing the message includes remaining as faithful as possible to the original Greek word order and sentence structure. The KJV, NASB and, to a lesser extent, the NRSV utilize this approach.

The *dynamic equivalence (or thought-for-thought) approach* tries to reproduce in the receptor language "the closest natural equivalent of the source-language message, first in terms of meaning and secondly in terms of style."[52] According to Nida and Taber, leading proponents of the dynamic equivalence approach, "reproducing the message" sums up the nature and goal of making a translation. The concern here is not merely to reproduce the wording

---

52. Eugene A. Nida and Charles R. Taber, *The Theory and Practice of Translation* (Leiden: E. J. Brill, 1969), 12.

and structure of the original, but to reproduce the message so that it has an equivalent effect on the modern reader. How far the translator can move away from the original wording and structure and still produce an equivalent effect on the modern reader is a matter of much debate. The NIV, REB, GNB, CEV, and the NLT are all examples of this second approach to translating.

Before making your finished translation, you also need to analyze your target audience since they constitute the primary users of the receptor (or target) language. What is their age range? What about their education level? How familiar is your audience with religious language? What do you know about their cultural background and their language capacity? As the translator you are the mediator between the ancient text and a modern audience, and you need to know as much as possible about both. Take a few minutes and jot down characteristics of your target audience to help focus your polished translation.

10.2— *Write an extended paraphrase of your passage.*

After polishing your translation, write an extended paraphrase of the passage. An extended paraphrase, as we envision it, gives you the opportunity to expand your translation and emphasize explicitly what you see as significant in the text. You have already translated the text, so don't repeat that step. Here you are crafting your own condensed commentary on the passage. Grant yourself the freedom to capture the passage's meaning in a way that connects with your audience. We predict that you will enjoy this as much as any part of the exegetical process.

Read through the examples below before making your own paraphrase. One is from Eugene Peterson, the other from one of our students. For the sake of comparison, we have placed a formal-equivalence translation just above each example.

Example → Literal translations and extended paraphrases:

- Matthew 5:33–37:

  "Again, you have heard that the ancients were told, 'You shall not make false vows, but shall fulfill your vows to the Lord.' But I say to you, make no oath at all, either by heaven, for it is the throne of God, or by the earth, for it is the footstool of His feet, or by Jerusalem, for it is the city of the great King. Nor shall you make an oath by your head, for you cannot make one hair white or black. But let your statements be 'Yes, yes' *or* 'No, no'; and anything beyond these is evil." (NASB)

  And don't say anything you don't mean. This counsel is embedded deep in our traditions. You only make things worse when you lay down a smoke screen of pious talk, saying 'I'll pray for you,' and never doing it, or saying 'God be with you,' and not meaning it. You don't make your words true by embellishing them with religious lace. In making your speech sound more religious, it becomes less true. Just say 'yes' and 'no.' When you manipulate words to get your own way, you go wrong. (Eugene Peterson, *The Message*)

- 1 Timothy 6:17–19:

  Instruct those who are rich in this present world not to be conceited or to fix their hope on the uncertainty of riches, but on God who richly supplies us with all things to enjoy. *Instruct them* to do good, to be rich in good works, to be generous and ready to share, storing up for themselves the treasure of a good foundation for the future, so that they may take hold of that which is life indeed. (NASB)

Tell the ones who have been blessed with wealth during their time on this earth not to have a proud or haughty attitude or to be foolish and deliberately let their hope rest on the uncertainty of all uncertainties: money. On the contrary, tell them to fix their hope on God. Why? Well, God is the one who richly and abundantly supplies us with all things in the first place. He is the Giver, and he wants us to enjoy all his gifts. As an outworking of their trust in God and his provision, tell the wealthy to do good things for others, and to do them in abundance, to be generous when sharing with others, and to always be ready and willing to share at a moment's notice. For the rich to give away their riches in this way is not to suffer loss, for they are storing up for themselves a different kind of treasure: the treasure of a good foundation for the coming age. Acquiring this treasure allows the wealthy to experience life, not this passing life, but the real thing: eternal life! (Nancy Day)

On Translating Scripture

Beekman, John, and John Callow. *Translating the Word of God*. Grand Rapids: Zondervan, 1974.

Brisco, Thomas V. "Translations and Hermeneutics." Pp. 190–202 in *Biblical Hermeneutics: A Comprehensive Introduction to Interpreting Scripture*. Ed. Bruce Corley, Steve Lemke, and Grant Lovejoy. Nashville: Broadman & Holman, 1996.

DeWaard, J., and Eugene A. Nida. *From One Language to Another: Functional Equivalence in Bible Translating*. Nashville: Nelson, 1986.

Eggar, Wilhelm. "Translation of the Text and Use of Translations." In *How to Read the New Testament: An Introduction to Linguistic and Historical-Critical Methodology*. Peabody, Mass.: Hendrickson, 1996.

Fee, Gordon D., and Douglas Stuart, "The Basic Tool: A Good Translation." In *How to Read the Bible for All Its Worth: A Guide to Understanding the Bible*, 2d ed. Grand Rapids: Zondervan, 1993.

Kubo, Sakae, and Walter F. Specht. *So Many Versions? 20ᵗʰ Century English Versions of the Bible*. Rev. ed. Grand Rapids: Zondervan, 1983.

Loewen, J. L. *The Practice of Translating*. New York: United Bible Society, 1981.

Louw, J. P. *Meaningful Translation: Its Implications for the Reader*. New York: United Bible Society, 1991.

Nida, Eugene A., and Charles R. Taber. *The Theory and Practice of Translation*. Leiden: E. J. Brill, 1969.

See also the separate volumes on specific books of the New Testament in the UBS Handbook Series.

Step 11—Application

Purpose →	To identify general principles conveyed by the passage and apply them to a modern audience

---

Overview of Step 11

11.1— Summarize the original situation or problem.

11.2— List the general principles communicated by the passage ("boiling down the truth").

11.3— Observe how the principles in the text address the original situation.

11.4— Identify a parallel situation in a modern context that contains all the key elements identified in Step 11.3.

11.5— Identify the various *areas* of life to which the passage might apply ("slicing up life").

11.6— Make specific application to the target audience ("primary life applications").

Application, sometimes referred to as "contextualization" (a term often used for applying the Bible in a cross-cultural context), stands as the main reason why most of us come to the pages of Scripture in the first place. We are eager to see how the Bible relates to our needs and problems, and rightly so. Oddly enough, application has sometimes suffered from neglect as interpreters have paid more attention to its neighbors with disciplines all their own—exegesis and homiletics. Grant Osborne puts it in proper perspective, however, when he notes, "It does little good to spend a great deal of time and energy exegeting a text properly only to throw it all away when we apply the text. If God's Word is any indicator, knowledge is inadequate unless it leads to action.... Proper contextualization is just as important as proper exegesis."[53]

To complicate matters, because of the gap between the world of the text and the world of today, application can be as confusing and challenging as it is exciting. For this reason we need a clear and reliable method for applying a passage of the New Testament to our lives, a method that builds on our understanding of the text and prepares us to communicate its message. Our method of application consists of six steps.[54] We will illustrate the method using Philippians 4:13, a much quoted but often misapplied text.

11.1—Summarize the original situation or problem.

For your own benefit, summarize what you have discovered (especially in Steps 2 and 7.3) about the original situation or problem. Whether you write your summary in paragraph form or make a list of the important factors, you want to set the key elements of the original situation clearly in front of you. You may want to start by describing the original situation behind the book before zeroing in on the more specific situation behind your passage.

---

53. Osborne, *Hermeneutical Spiral*, 338.

54. Our six-step approach to applying a passage draws heavily on the models suggested by Grant Osborne (*The Hermeneutical Spiral*, 336–38), Klein, Blomberg, and Hubbard (*Introduction to Biblical Interpretation*, 406–7), and Jack Kuhatschek, *Applying the Bible* (Grand Rapids: Zondervan, 1996).

Example → Summary of the original situation behind Philippians 4:13:

> The apostle Paul is in prison and awaiting trial (1:7, 13–14, 17). He pens the letter to the Philippians during a trying time in his life that resulted from his faithfulness to Christ in the ministry of the gospel. Paul's reasons for writing reflect the nature of the letter as a "hortatory letter of friendship."[55] The element of "friendship" appears in the return of Epaphroditus, Paul's report about his own situation, and his desire to thank the Philippians for their ministry to him. The "hortatory" element appears in his call for the Philippians to stand firm in the face of external opposition and his warning against internal unrest.
>
> With regard to Philippians 4:10–13, Paul is writing to acknowledge their monetary gift sent through Epaphroditus, but also to communicate to them that his ministry is not ultimately dependent on such a gift. He is not ungrateful, but simply dependent on Christ for the ministry of the gospel.

11.2—*List the general principles communicated by the passage ("boiling down the truth").*

In many ways this step marks the climax of the exegetical task (i.e., the discovery of the original meaning of a text) and the transition to application and exposition. Here you are beginning to bridge the gap between the world of the text and the world of today. This step represents a crucial necessity because Scripture is both timely and timeless, as the editors of *The NIV Application Commentary* series remind us:

> God's Word is *timely*. The authors of Scripture spoke to specific situations, problems, and questions. Paul warned the Galatians about the consequences of circumcision and the dangers of trying to be justified by law (Gal. 5:2–5) . . . . The timely nature of Scripture enables us to hear God's Word in situations that were *concrete* rather than abstract.
>
> Yet the timely nature of Scripture also creates problems. Our situations, difficulties, and questions are not always directly related to those faced by the people in the Bible. Therefore, God's word to them does not always seem relevant to us. For example, when was the last time someone urged you to be circumcised, claiming that it was a necessary part of justification . . . ?
>
> Fortunately, Scripture is not only timely, but *timeless*. Just as God spoke to the original audience, so he still speaks to us through the pages of Scripture. Because we share a common humanity with the people in the Bible, we discover a *universal dimension* in the problems they faced and the solutions God gave them. The timeless nature of Scripture enables it to speak with power in every time and in every culture.[56]

When you identify the general truths or principles conveyed by a passage, you are discerning what is timeless in your passage. Step 11.2 is indeed foundational! You cannot apply and communicate the great truths of God's Word unless you first identify them. Before continuing on with our example from Philippians 4:13, we need to say more about how to locate general principles in your passage.

In his book *Applying the Bible*, Jack Kuhatschek recommends that you ask three questions to find the general principles in a passage.[57]

> 1. *Does the author state a general principle?*

---

55. Gordon D. Fee, *Paul's Letter to the Philippians*, 34.
56. From p. 8 of the "Series Introduction" in *The NIV Application Commentary*.
57. Kuhatschek, *Applying the Bible*, 57–61.

Begin by looking to see if the passage clearly states a general principle. When Paul discusses the topic of food sacrificed to idols in 1 Corinthians 8, he supplies a principle in verse 9: "Be careful, however, that the exercise of your freedom does not become a stumbling block to the weak." In 1 Timothy 6:10 we read that the love of money is a root of all kinds of evil. In Ephesians 6:2 children are told to honor their father and mother. In Hebrews 10:25 believers are warned not to give up meeting together. In these and many other cases in the New Testament, the general principle appears on the surface of the passage.

2. *Does the broader context reveal a general principle?*

   Next, look to see if the author supplies a principle in the broader context. The command for slaves to obey their earthly masters in Ephesians 6:5 turns out to be an example of the general principle stated in 5:21: "Submit to one another out of reverence for Christ." In this case you locate the general principle by examining the broader context.

3. *Why was this specific command or instruction given?*

   Sometimes you will find the principle not on the surface, but in the underlying reason. Try to discover the *reason* behind the command or set of instructions. When Paul warns against circumcision in Galatians 5:2–3, we need to know why. And don't be surprised if you have to ask why more than once:

   • Don't seek to be circumcised. Why?
   • Because no one will be justified by keeping the law. Why?
   • Because no one can earn God's acceptance by human effort, but must accept it as a grace gift by faith.

Kuhatschek's guidelines are dependable especially when working in epistolary literature. (Notice that all the example texts cited above are from New Testament letters.) But what about trying to identify principles in other types of literature? Here you may need to review what you learned in Step 3.1, where you read about how to interpret different kinds of New Testament literature. The important question is this: How does a particular literary type communicate meaning?

Since over 50 percent of the New Testament is narrative, we would like to suggest a few more helps for identifying principles in that kind of literature. That is not to say that the above questions are of no value when looking for general principles in a story, just that you may find some additional guidelines useful. You should know also that we are not trying to reduce or flatten the narrative to a list of abstract propositional statements. Stories tend to transport worldviews more powerfully and holistically than isolated abstract statements.[58] But neither should we avoid altogether trying to analyze and summarize a story's meaning. In his book, *A Basic Guide to Interpreting the Bible*, Robert Stein offers solid principles for interpreting biblical narrative:[59]

   • Look for clues in an author's introduction and conclusion to the story:

      "Jesus did many other miraculous signs in the presence of his disciples, which are not recorded in this book. But these are written that you may believe that Jesus is

---

58. For an insightful discussion on "The Nature of Stories," see N. T. Wright, *The New Testament and the People of God* (Minneapolis: Augsburg-Fortress, 1992), 69–80.

59. Stein, *Interpreting the Bible*, 157–66. Most of the examples cited below are used by Stein in his discussion.

the Christ, the Son of God, and that by believing you may have life in his name." (John 20:30–31)

Another example appears in Acts 2:42–47, the explanatory conclusion to the events described in Acts 2.

- Look for comments inserted directly into the narrative by the author to help the reader understand how they should interpret the story:

  In the narrative about clean and unclean foods in Mark 7:1–23, Mark adds this comment in verse 19: "In saying this, Jesus declared all foods 'clean.'" This parenthetical remark reveals Mark's understanding of the primary significance of Jesus' teaching.

- Look for repetition of key themes. John Polhill views repetition as the key for finding theology in the narrative of Acts:

  Acts is basically narrative, and its "theology" is to be found primarily there. What are the recurrent themes in the episodes? What motifs dominate the movement of the story line? This is where the "theology" of Acts really lies. It is a "narrative theology."[60]

- Look carefully at points where the story shifts to direct discourse (where conversation is signified by quotation marks in the English text and a capital letter preceded by a comma in UBS[4]):

  In the story of Jesus' stilling the storm at the end of Mark 4, the question and comment by the disciples is especially significant: "Who is this? Even the wind and the waves obey him!" (4:41).

Now that we have given you some idea about how to find general principles, let's return to our example and show you a general principle from Philippians 4:13. When writing out a general principle, you may find it helpful at first to put down a statement that keeps everything in the first century. Notice how the first statement in the example below ("Paul tells . . . ") makes for an easy transition to the timeless truth captured by the second statement ("Christ will . . . ").

Example → A general principle communicated by Philippians 4:13:

First-century statement: Paul tells the Philippians that he has learned to be content in a variety of circumstances through Christ, who gives him strength.

General principle: Believers can learn to be content in a variety of circumstances through Christ, who gives them strength.

Another attempt at a general principle: Christ will give believers strength to be content in a variety of trying circumstances that come as a result of following him faithfully.

11.3—Observe how the principles in the text address the original situation.

Seeing the intersection between the original situation and the biblical text stands at the heart of the application process. In this intersection you will find certain key elements. And these key elements constitute the core of the encounter between the answers and solutions in the text and the questions and problems in the situation.

---

60. John B. Polhill, *Acts* (Nashville: Broadman, 1992), 54

Example → The principle in Philippians 4:13 meets the original situation:

As the principle in the text intersects with the historical situation, several key elements emerge:

- A Christian
- A Christian who is experiencing a variety of trying circumstances as a result of following Christ faithfully
- Christ will enable the Christian to be content whatever the circumstances

Now that we have identified these key elements resulting from the intersection between the situation and the text, we are ready to make a connection with the modern world and apply the meaning of the passage to our lives.

11.4—*Discover a parallel situation in a modern context that contains all the key elements identified in Step 11.3.*

Here we are building a bridge to connect the ancient text with the modern world. The key is to find a modern situation that contains *all* (not just a few) of the key elements identified in the previous step. As Jack Kuhatschek puts it, "if we omit one or more of these key elements . . . we are no longer really applying the principle found in the passage."[61]

Often as interpreters we intuitively associate a truth or principle with a particular text without paying careful attention to whether it contains *all* the key elements. The principle that interests us may indeed be biblical (i.e., intended by some passage in Scripture), but may not be a truth communicated by this particular passage. This is the question of the hour: Does this passage teach this particular truth?

In the contrasting scenarios below we hope to illustrate the crucial need to find a parallel modern situation that contains all the key elements.

Example → An apparent parallel for Philippians 4:13 *without* all the key elements (thus a poor application of the text):

As we said before, to be a true parallel we must find all the key elements, not just a few of them. As you may know, in American society Philippians 4:13 has become a popular theme verse for Christian athletes. For instance, on the robe of a recent championship boxer, Philippians 4:13 was stitched boldly for all to see. We suspect that the verse supplied the boxer with encouragement to fight hard in order to win the match. In that context the phrase "I can do everything" undoubtedly refers to either defeating his opponent or doing his best in athletic competition. Assuming that both Paul and the boxer are Christians and both look to Christ for strength, key elements of the intersection between the original situation and the biblical text are still missing.

The apostle Paul and the boxer have radically different understandings of the expression, "I can do everything." The literary context makes it clear that "everything" refers to a variety of trying circumstances. At this particular time in Paul's life, the pendulum was swinging toward a trial of "need" rather than a trial of "plenty." The term "do" refers to a learned contentment rather than a conquering ability. There is a world of difference between the "trials" of athletic competition and of being imprisoned for your faith. One awaits a final bell or a finish line, the other a possible execution.

---

61. *Applying the Bible*, 73.

When key elements of the intersection between the situation and the text are ignored or omitted, passages like Philippians 4:13 are misapplied. Misapplications should be avoided because they ultimately hurt people by enslaving them! The substantive principle of contentment in Christ whatever the circumstances gives way to a superficial proof text for God to help us conquer our opponent in a game of some sort. What happens when there are Christians on the other team quoting (or misquoting) the same verse? What happens when the game is no longer boxing or soccer or basketball, but real life?

Example → A parallel for Philippians 4:13 *with* all the key elements:

> As a student you may be experiencing, or know someone who is experiencing, financial difficulty. It may be that you had all your needs met when you lived at home but now struggle to make ends meet. The long hours of work translate into late nights of study and sleepy mornings in class. You believe that God has called you to academic preparation, but this circumstance is difficult, you are often fatigued, and your spiritual life even seems to be affected. The principle of Philippians 4:13 suggests that Christ gives strength for us to deal with such difficult circumstances, enabling us to find contentment through him.

Finding a parallel that possesses all the key elements helps ensure our submission to the text and prevent any selfish misappropriation of the text on our part. Those of us who uphold the full authority of Scripture with various theological declarations should also be careful to uphold its authority when it comes to the process of making practical application.

You may be concerned that the method may restrict the application process. We see no need to worry. God's Word is relevant! You will normally find numerous parallel situations in a modern context with all the key elements. When you find a modern parallel that contains all the key elements, you can be confident that you are applying what the biblical text really means.

11.5—Identify the various areas of life to which the passage might apply ("slicing up life").

Take a moment and think of the various areas of life to which the passage might apply. Such areas might be home, job, school, friendships, or others. This step will help you think creatively about various situations that could be addressed by the principles from your passage. The circle on your exegetical worksheet for Step 11 can be divided like a pizza into different "slices." Write the areas you thought of in those parts of the circle as follows:

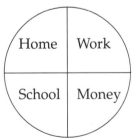

11.6—Make specific application to the target audience ("primary life applications").

You have already started this process in a general sense in the preceding steps. In this the final phase of application try to move beyond generalizations to specific applications of the passage to your target audience. In light of your passage, think for a moment about the specific life needs of your audience and list a few of them. When we say "in light of your passage," we are talking mainly about the key elements you identified in Step 11.3. Think about people in your audience whose life situations contain these key elements.

Example → Life needs of a hypothetical audience in light of Philippians 4:13:

- A large family experiences financial hardship because they are called to a ministry that barely meets their needs.
- A single mother whose non-Christian husband recently deserted her because of her faith struggles to trust Christ for strength.
- A young professional tries to maintain perspective when he suddenly finds himself making more money than he ever imagined he would make.

Identifying the life needs of people in your audience requires that you be involved in their lives. It takes time and energy to get to know people and their needs, interests, convictions, questions, and problems. But make no mistake, it will be worth your effort!

In light of all you have learned about the passage and the life needs of your audience, make specific applications. And, as Grant Osborne notes, don't forget the "how":

> The average preacher or teacher lives in an idealistic world of "what" or "why," simply pointing to the theological principle behind a text and directly addressing the audience with it. However, the average congregation or class lives in a different world, with many obstacles providing a barrier between the realization of need and the achievement of practical change in their lives. Every person needs to discover not only "what" but "how"! The preacher therefore should suggest practical ways by which the individual can discover the application and put it to work in concrete daily situations.[62]

In the case of Philippians 4:13, your application might specify particular ways that Christ enables his people to be content when they encounter trying circumstances. Your audience will then have some idea of how they can expect to experience the strength of Christ and learn contentment when following Christ takes them into trying circumstances.

Application (or Contextualization)

Fee, Gordon D., and Douglas Stuart. *How to Read the Bible for All Its Worth*. 2d ed. Grand Rapids: Zondervan, 1993.

Gilliland, Dean S., ed. *The Word Among Us: Contexualizing Theology for Mission Today*. Dallas: Word, 1989.

Hesselgrave, David J., and Edward Rommen. *Contextualization: Meaning, Methods, and Models*. Grand Rapids: Baker, 1989.

Johnson, Elliott E. *Expository Hermeneutics: An Introduction*. Grand Rapids: Zondervan, 1990.

*Klein, William W., Craig L. Blomberg, and Robert L. Hubbard. *Introduction to Biblical Interpretation*. Dallas: Word, 1993. (See esp. pp. 401–26.)

*Kuhatschek, Jack. *Applying the Bible*. Grand Rapids: Zondervan, 1996.

Larkin, William J., Jr. *Culture and Biblical Hermeneutics: Interpreting and Applying the Authoritative Word in a Relativistic Age*. Lanham, Md.: Univ. Press of America, 1993.

*Osborne, Grant R. *The Hermeneutical Spiral: A Comprehensive Introduction to Biblical Interpretation*. Downers Grove: InterVarsity, 1991. (See esp. pp. 318–65.)

Thiselton, Anthony C. *New Horizons in Hermeneutics*. Grand Rapids: Zondervan, 1992.

---

62. Osborne, *Hermeneutical Spiral*, 349.

Step 12—Preaching/
Teaching Outline

> **Purpose** → To develop an outline for use in preaching or teaching that is both biblical and relevant

---
Overview of Step 12

12.1— Retrieve your provisional outline and revise it based on what you discovered in Steps 7–11.

12.2— Craft your outline to a form suitable for communication.

12.3— Prepare your own heart to preach or teach the biblical message.

Homiletics—the study of the preparation and delivery of sermons—is a field that has received no small amount of attention. There are a number of excellent guides to crafting a sermon, and we encourage you to read widely in this area (see the bibliography). All we can hope to do in this final step is give you a few basic suggestions for shaping an outline to use in communicating your passage.

There are a variety of ways to shape a sermon, and certainly not all sermons must stick closely to the structure of the text. But in our view the form of the sermon should mirror the form of the text in substantive ways.[63] By building on your provisional outline, an outline that already reflects the semantic structure of the text, you can be confident that your preaching/teaching outline will also clearly reflect the text's structure.

12.1—*Retrieve your provisional outline and revise it based on what you discovered in Steps 7–11*

Begin by retrieving your provisional outline from Step 6. This outline will serve as a dependable starting point to crafting a preaching/teaching outline.

In all likelihood you will find it necessary to make some adjustments to your provisional outline in light of what you have learned since Step 6. By "adjustments" we mean anything from wholesale changes in content to slight alterations in wording. Pay particular attention to your polished translation and extended paraphrase (Step 10), since they capture concisely your own understanding of the passage. Don't be concerned yet with crafting a preaching/teaching outline, just focus on updating the content of your exegetical outline. Once you are comfortable with the outline's content, you will be ready to shape it into a form suitable for communication.

Example → Provisional outline of James 1:2–4:

    1:2–3 Consider it joy when you encounter trials

        1:2a Command → consider it pure joy

---

63. See the insightful article by Grant Lovejoy, "Shaping Sermons by the Literary Form of the Text," in Corley, Lemke and Lovejoy, *Biblical Hermeneutics*, 318–39. While recognizing that the two are strongly connected, we emphasize the semantic structure of the text more than its literary form in shaping the sermon.

1:2b   Time → whenever you encounter trials of various kinds
1:3   Reason → because you know that the testing of your faith produces endurance

1:4   Let endurance finish its work

1:4a   Command → let endurance finish its work
1:4b   Intended Result → that you may be mature and complete

12.2—*Craft your outline to a form suitable for communication*

Now you must turn your attention to making an impact on a real audience, perhaps the same audience you envisioned in the application phase (see Step 11). Use the following guidelines for crafting your revised outline into a form suitable for use in preaching and teaching.

a. What is the main purpose of the sermon or lesson?

Whether you call this a thesis statement or central idea or something else, you need to capture in one sentence the heart of what you want to communicate to your audience. As Harold Bryson says, "A sermon needs to have a point before it has points."[64] As you look carefully at your existing outline, come up with a single statement that accurately and clearly reflects the big idea of the passage.[65]

Example → The central idea for a sermon based on James 1:2–4:

Christians should receive trials with joy because of the benefit to their character.

b. What response do you expect from the people?

What do you want people to do as a result of hearing you speak; or, if you prefer, what do you want your preaching/teaching to do in the lives of the people who hear it? How do you want people to feel, think, or act as a result of what you communicate?[66] Try completing the following sentence as a way of stating the response you expect: "When people hear this sermon or lesson, I want them to _____." Is the expected response specific enough? Is it realistic? Does it connect with the audience? Is it faithful to the biblical text?

Example → Expected response from a sermon based on James 1:2–4:

When people hear this message, I want them to determine to allow God to shape their character in the midst of trying circumstances rather than changing their circumstances.

c. Do you need to reshape your outline to enhance communication?

We are encouraging you to develop an outline for use in preaching and teaching that closely reflects the semantic structure of the biblical text. Even so, some reshaping might be in order in light of your main purpose and expected response, both reflections of the life situation of your audience.

---

64. Harold T. Bryson, *Expository Preaching: The Art of Preaching Through a Book of the Bible* (Nashville: Broadman & Holman, 1995), 320.

65. See the helpful chapter entitled "What's the Big Idea?" in Haddon W. Robinson, *Biblical Preaching: The Development and Delivery of Expository Messages* (Grand Rapids: Baker, 1980), 31–48.

66. Bryson, *Expository Preaching*, 322.

An outline is suitable for communication when it is both biblical and relevant. Grant Osborne notes the common tendency to make these mutually exclusive concerns:

> Too often preachers stress one side or the other, so that the sermon becomes either dry exposition or dynamic entertainment. Both spheres, the original meaning of the text and the modern significance for our context, are critical in expository preaching, the true goal of the hermeneutical enterprise.[67]

In our view, Scripture has inherent relevance, but we must expose that relevance to a modern audience that often possesses little connection to the original context. For this reason rephrasing the points in your outline or reshaping the outline itself may be appropriate.

Example → Sermon outline for James 1:2–4:

"Responding to Trials"

Trials are sure to come our way (1:2b)
We should receive trials with joy (1:2a)
We can rejoice because we know the intended result of our trials (1:3–4)

d. Develop each point in the outline with supporting elements.

There are a number of supporting elements available for expanding your outline, including explanation, argumentation, illustration, and application.[68] Below each point in your preaching/teaching outline list the supporting elements you think you need along with a brief statement about how each element will function in your sermon or lesson.

Example → Sermon outline for James 1:2–4 with supporting elements:

"Responding to Trials"

Trials are sure to come our way (1:2b)

Expl → What does James mean by "trial"?
Illus/Appl → Christians can react to trials in a variety of ways
Expl → The nature of "encountering trials of various kinds"
Appl → Help Christians accept the certainty of testing times

We should receive trials with joy (1:2a)

Expl/Illus → The difference between biblical "joy" and worldly "happiness"
Appl → Making trials an occasion for joy
Expl/Appl → It is natural to ask "Why?" when facing trials

We can rejoice because we know the intended result of our trials (1:3–4)

Expl → We can know that testing produces endurance
Expl → Endurance yields a fully developed Christian character
Appl → Determine not to short-circuit the process of testing

---

67. Osborne, *Hermeneutical Spiral*, 12.
68. See chapter 14 in Bryson, *Expository Preaching*, for a full discussion of each of these elements and others. See also Robinson's chapter "Making Dry Bones Live" in *Biblical Preaching*, 137–55.

e. Include transition statements.

Transitions should be brief, simple statements. They serve two purposes: First, they give cohesiveness to the outline by linking together the main points. Second, they facilitate progression by enabling the listener to follow the movement from one main part to the next.

Osborne suggests three parts to an effective transition statement:

- a concise summary of a previous section—e.g., "We have seen how Jesus taught that God's forgiveness is conditional on our willingness to forgive"
- a connecting phrase—e.g., "and now we will turn to the letters"
- the introduction of the next point—e.g., "in order to see what they say about forgiveness."[69]

Write out transition statements between each main point in your outline. After you develop your introduction and conclusion, add transition statements linking those to the body of the outline.

f. Add an introduction and a conclusion.[70]

By saving your introduction and conclusion for last, you will know better what you want to communicate and have a better idea of how you should begin and end. We suggest that you write out a brief paragraph indicating how you plan to introduce and conclude your sermon or lesson.

Working through the following questions will help you achieve an effective **introduction**:

- How do you want to gain the audience's attention?
- How will you cause people's needs to surface so that the message of the text can meet them?
- How do you plan on presenting the basic idea of the sermon?
- How will you make them aware of the larger biblical context so they will have a framework for understanding the teaching?

In the **conclusion** you want to summarize the heart of your teaching and drive home the main point so that the people are motivated to feel differently, think differently, or act differently. (Remember your statement of expected response?) Imagine your audience asking the question, So what? They want to know the difference your message will make in their lives and now is the time to tell them.

After crafting a suitable outline, there is only one thing to do before preaching the sermon or teaching the lesson: prepare your own heart.

12.4—*Prepare your own heart to preach or teach.*

We conclude our discussion of the twelve-step exegetical method by looking briefly at the second of our "spiritual preparation" bookends (see Step 1). Just as we prepared our hearts to interpret in Step 1, now we prepare our hearts to communicate what God has graciously allowed us to understand. Most of what we said in Step 1 applies here as well.

---

69. Osborne, *Hermeneutical Spiral*, 360.

70. Haddon Robinson offers helpful advice in formulating an introduction and a conclusion in his chapter "Start with a Bang and Quit All Over" (*Biblical Preaching*, 159–73).

In our age of busyness and information overload, we desperately need a sustained reflection on the message of the biblical text. We need time for God's Word to sink deep into our hearts and minds and have its effect. What's more, our audience needs this to take place in the lives of their preacher or teacher. As Grant Osborne points out, in preaching and teaching God desires to work *through* his servants:

> Sermon preparation must be a devotional exercise (a first-person encounter) before it becomes a proclamation event (a second-person encounter). Preachers continually must place themselves before the text rather than merely place themselves behind the text in order to direct it to this or that situation in the church.[71]

How can we ask people to do what we are unwilling to do? Before you communicate a message to an audience, to take time to allow that message to do its work in your own life. You might want to write out a short prayer, asking God to work the truth of the text deep into your life so that your words reflect his character.

Homiletics

Adam, Peter. *Speaking God's Words: A Practical Theology of Expository Preaching.* Downers Grove: Inter Varsity, 1998.

Brown, H. C., et al. *Steps to the Sermon: Revised Edition.* Nashville: Broadman & Holman, 1996.

Bryson, Harold T. *Expository Preaching: The Art of Preaching Through a Book of the Bible.* Nashville: Broadman & Holman, 1995.

Chapell, Brian. *Christ-Centered Preaching: Redeeming the Expository Sermon.* Grand Rapids: Baker, 1994.

Cox, James W. *Biblical Preaching: An Expositor's Treasury.* Philadelphia: Westminster, 1983.

Fasol, Al. *Essentials for Biblical Preaching.* Grand Rapids: Baker, 1989.

Greidanus, Sidney. *The Modern Preacher and the Ancient Text: Interpreting and Preaching Biblical Literature.* Grand Rapids: Eerdmans, 1988.

Long, Thomas G. *Preaching and the Literary Forms of the Bible.* Philadelphia: Fortress, 1989.

MacArthur, John F., Jr., Richard L. Mayhue, and Robert L. Thomas. *Rediscovering Expository Preaching.* Dallas: Word, 1992.

McDill, Wayne. *The Twelve Essential Skills for Great Preaching.* Nashville: Broadman & Holman, 1994.

Miller, Calvin. *The Empowered Communicator: Seven Keys to Unlocking an Audience.* Nashville: Broadman & Holman, 1994.

Osborne, Grant R. *The Hermeneutical Spiral: A Comprehensive Introduction to Biblical Interpretation.* Downers Grove: InterVarsity, 1991. (See esp. pp. 339–65.)

Robinson, Haddon W. *Biblical Preaching: The Development and Delivery of Expository Messages.* Grand Rapids: Baker, 1980.

Stott, John R. W. *Between Two Worlds: The Art of Preaching in the Twentieth Century.* Grand Rapids: Eerdmans, 1982.

---

71. Osborne, *Hermeneutical Spiral*, 344.

Appendix A

Student's Syntax Summary[1]

---

1. The following outline is from the partial summary of Wallace's *Greek Grammar Beyond the Basics* in Bill Mounce's *Graded Reader*, 141–82.

CASE

Nominative

- Subject Nominative
- Predicate Nominative
- Nominative in Simple Apposition
- Nominative Absolute
- Pendent Nominative
- Parenthetic Nominative
- Nominative for Vocative (Nominative of Address)
- Nominative of Exclamation
- Nominative of Appellation

Vocative

- Simple Address
- Emphatic (Emotional) Address

Genitive

- Descriptive Genitive
- Possessive Genitive
- Genitive of Relationship
- Partitive (Wholative) Genitive
- Attributive Genitive
- Attributed Genitive
- Genitive of Material
- Genitive of Content
- Genitive in Simple Apposition
- Genitive of Apposition (Epexegetical)
- Genitive of Subordination
- Ablatival Genitive of Separation
- Ablatival Genitive of Comparison
- Subjective Genitive
- Objective Genitive
- Plenary Genitive
- Genitive of Time
- Genitive of Association
- Genitive after Certain Verbs (as Direct Object)
- Genitive after Certain Adjectives and Adverbs

Dative

- Dative of Indirect Object
- Dative of Interest
- Dative of Reference/Respect
- Dative in Simple Apposition
- Local Dative of Sphere
- Local Dative of Time
- Instrumental Dative of Association (Accompaniment)

- Instrumental Dative of Manner
- Instrumental Dative of Means/Instrument
- Instrumental Dative of Measure/Degree of Difference
- Instrumental Dative of Cause
- Dative of Direct Object
- Dative after Certain Nouns
- Dative after Certain Adjectives

Accusative

- Accusative of Direct Object
- Double Accusative
- Predicate Accusative
- Accusative Subject of the Infinitive
- Accusative in Simple Apposition
- Accusative of Manner
- Accusative of Measure
- Accusative of Respect or (General) Reference

THE ARTICLE

As a Pronoun

- Personal Pronoun
- Relative Pronoun
- Possessive Pronoun

With Substantives

- Simple Identification
- Anaphoric (Previous Reference)
- Deictic ("Pointing")
- Par Excellence
- Monadic ("One of a Kind" or "Unique")
- Well-Known ("Celebrity")
- Abstract (Article with Abstract Nouns)
- Generic (Categorical)

As a Substantive

As a Function Marker

- To Denote Adjectival Positions
- With Possessive Pronouns
- In Genitive Phrases
- With Indeclinable Nouns
- With Participles
- With Demonstratives
- With Nominative Nouns
- To Distinguish Subject from Predicate Nominative and Object from Complement

Absence of the Article

- Indefinite
- Qualitative
- Definite

VOICE

Active Voice

- Simple Active
- Causative Active
- Stative Active
- Reflexive Active

Middle Voice

- Direct Middle
- Indirect Middle
- Causative Middle
- Permissive Middle
- Deponent Middle

Passive Voice

- Simple Passive
- Deponent Passive

MOOD

Indicative

- Declarative Indicative
- Interrogative Indicative
- Conditional Indicative
- Potential Indicative
- Cohortative (Command) Indicative

Subjunctive

- Hortatory Subjunctive
- Deliberative Subjunctive
- Emphatic Negation Subjunctive
- Prohibitive Subjunctive
- Subjunctive in Conditional Sentences
- Ἵνα + the Subjunctive
- Subjunctive with Verbs of Fearing, etc.
- Subjunctive in Indirect Questions
- Subjunctive in Indefinite Relative Clause
- Subjunctive in Indefinite Temporal Clause

Optative

- Voluntative Optative
- Potential Optative

Imperative

- Command Imperative
- Prohibition Imperative
- Request (Entreaty) Imperative
- Permissive Imperative
- As a Stereotyped Greeting

TENSES

Present

- Instantaneous (Aoristic) Present
- Progressive (Descriptive) Present
- Extending-from-the Past Present
- Iterative Present
- Customary (Habitual) Present
- Gnomic Present
- Historical (Dramatic) Present
- Futuristic Present
- Present Retained in Indirect Discourse

Imperfect

- Progressive (Descriptive) Imperfect
- Ingressive (Inchoative, Inceptive) Imperfect
- Iterative Imperfect
- Customary (Habitual) Imperfect
- Conative (Voluntative, Tendential) Imperfect
- Imperfect Retained in Indirect Discourse

Future

- Predictive Future
- Imperatival Future
- Deliberative Future
- Gnomic Future

Aorist

- Constative Aorist
- Ingressive (Inceptive, Inchoative) Aorist
- Consummative (Culminative) Aorist
- Gnomic Aorist
- Epistolary Aorist
- Proleptic (Futuristic) Aorist
- Immediate Past (Dramatic) Aorist

Perfect

- Intensive (Resultative) Perfect
- Extensive (Consummative) Perfect
- Perfect with a Present Force

Pluperfect

- Intensive (Resultative) Pluperfect
- Extensive (Consummative) Pluperfect

INFINITIVE

Adverbial Uses

- Purpose
- Result
- Time
- Cause
- Means
- Complementary

Substantival Uses

- Subject
- Direct Object
- Indirect Discourse
- Appositional
- Epexegetical

PARTICIPLE

Adjectival Participles

- Adjectival (Dependent)
- Substantival (Independent)

Verbal Participles

- Adverbial Temporal
- Adverbial Manner
- Adverbial Means
- Adverbial Cause
- Adverbial Condition
- Adverbial Concession
- Adverbial Purpose (Telic)
- Adverbial Result
- Attendant Circumstance
- Periphrastic
- Redundant (Pleonastic)
- Independent Verbal Participle as an Imperative
- Genitive Absolute

Appendix B

Worksheets for the Exegetical Method

General Introduction & Literary Context

List and number your sources:

Steps 2 & 3

Reference:

Parsing

v.	Word	Tns	Vce	Md	Pr	No	Cs	Gn	No	Lexical Form	Syntax	Translation

Prov. Trans.

notes on textual variants:

additional syntax notes:

Reference:

Grammatical and Semantic Structure

Reference:

Provisional Outline

Word Study

Reference:

Lexical Analysis:

Cross References:

(word)

Lexical Analysis:

Cross References:

(word)

Lexical Analysis:

Cross References:

(word)

List and number your sources:

Broader Biblical & Theological Contexts

Reference:

notes keyed to the sources below:

List and number your sources

Commentaries and Special Studies

notes keyed to the sources below:

List and number your sources

Reference:

Step 9

Extended Paraphrase

Finished Translation

Reference:

Slicing Up Life

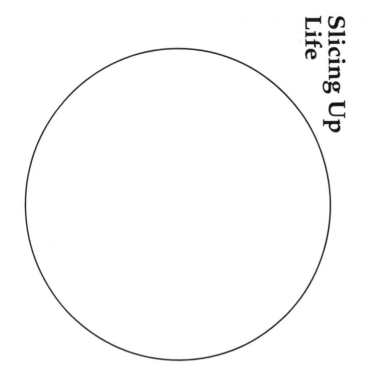

Primary Life Application

Boiling Down Truth

Reference:

Reference:

For additional textbooks on New Testament Greek look for these outstanding titles:

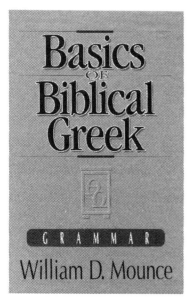

Basics of Biblical Greek
Grammar and Workbook
William D. Mounce

Basics of Biblical Greek takes an integrated approach to teaching and learning New Testament Greek. Students immediately start working with verses from the New Testament, tying the lessons directly to the biblical text. It makes learning Greek a natural process and shows from the very beginning how an understanding of Greek helps in understanding the New Testament. Written from the student's perspective, this approach combines the best of the deductive and inductive methods. The workbook features a parsing section and is usefully perforated with hole-punched pages for loose-leaf binders.

Grammar (Hardcover): 0-310-59800-1
Workbook (Softcover): 0-310-40091-0

Greek Grammar Beyond the Basics
An Exegetical Syntax of the New Testament
Daniel B. Wallace

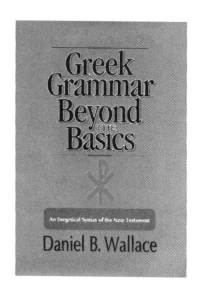

Depth, accuracy, relevancy, and up-to-date presentation make this intermediate Greek grammar the finest available—equipping students of the New Testament with the skills they need to do biblical exegesis. Written by a world-class authority on Greek grammar, it links grammar and exegesis to provide today's student, expositor, or professor with solid exegetical and linguistic foundations.

Greek Grammar Beyond the Basics integrates the technical requirements for proper Greek interpretation with the actual interests and needs of Bible students. It is the first truly exegetical syntax in which the author constantly has an eye on the role of syntax in exegesis.

Hardcover: 0-310-37340-9

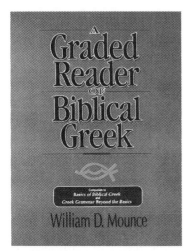

A Graded Reader of Biblical Greek

Companion to Basics of Biblical Greek and Greek Grammar Beyond the Basics

William D. Mounce

This multipurpose volume serves as a companion to *Basics of Biblical Greek*, *Greek Grammar Beyond the Basics*, and *Biblical Greek Exegesis*. It contains annotated readings from the New Testament designed for second-year Greek students. Sections from the Greek New Testament are presented in order of increasing difficulty, and unfamiliar forms and constructions are annotated.

Softcover: 0-310-20582-4

The Morphology of Biblical Greek

A Companion to Basics of Biblical Greek and
An Analytical Lexicon to the Greek New Testament

William D. Mounce

The Morphology of Biblical Greek shows how Greek word forms (even the most "irregular" ones) are derived by means of a limited set of rules. It explains why Greek words "do what they do" in a way that second-year Greek students can understand. It also includes paradigms, principal parts, and an index of all words in the New Testament with their morphological category.

Hardcover: 0-310-41040-1

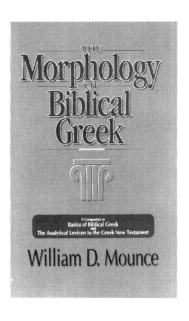

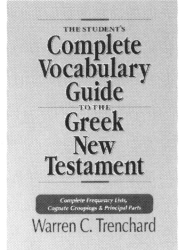

The Student's Complete Vocabulary Guide to the Greek New Testament

Complete Frequency Lists, Cognate Groupings, and Principal Parts

Warren C. Trenchard

The Student's Complete Vocabulary Guide to the Greek New Testament is the most complete book of its kind. Designed for both reference and study, it covers the entire vocabulary of the Greek New Testament—not just the words that occur most frequently. Words are arranged by frequency and in a separate section by cognates. Principal parts for all verbs found in the New Testament are also listed. A new revised edition being published October 1998 adds the Goodrick-Kohlenberger numbers to the index.

Softcover: 0-310-22695-3

Available at your local Christian or college bookstore

ZondervanPublishingHouse

Grand Rapids, Michigan

http://www.zondervan.com

A Division of HarperCollinsPublishers